# Evaluation of Management Training

A practical framework, with cases,
for evaluating training needs and results

by PETER WARR
MICHAEL BIRD and NEIL RACKHAM

Gower Press

First published in Britain by Gower Press Limited
140 Great Portland Street, London W1N 5TA
1970

Second impression 1971

ISBN 0 7161 0049 5

Printed in  Britain by Lowe & Brydone (Printers) Limited, London

# EVALUATION OF MANAGEMENT TRAINING

A Gower Press Special Study

# A Gower Press Special Study

# Contents

# Illustrations

# Introduction

The importance of evaluation in the training process is constantly
emphasised. Trainers are frequently reminded by various authorities
that they should investigate the effects of their training programmes,
and this same idea is impressed upon new recruits to the profession
at a very early stage in their training careers. Most trainers
accept the need for evaluation, but this is not by any means the
same as knowing how to set about it. Unfortunately exhortation
has not been followed by an equivalent amount of practical guidance,
and this lack of practical procedural advice is particularly
apparent in the case of supervisory and management training.
The principal aim of this book is not to make the case for
evaluation, but instead to offer some suggestions as to how
it can be accomplished.

However, right at the outset let us briefly state some reasons
why we believe evaluation will help the trainer. We see three
major advantages, as follows:

1    Evaluation provides the trainer with information that will
enable him to increase the effectiveness of later or even
current training. Deprived of information about the results
of a training sequence there is no logical way in which the
trainer can plan the more effective utilisation of his
resources. It only becomes possible to learn by experience
if successes can be distinguished from failures.

2    The training department, like all other departments, will
be expected to play its part in the achievement of the
organisation's objectives. If trainers can demonstrate
factually that they are making a genuine contribution
to organisational goals, this can lead to an increase in
both the standing and influence of the training department
within that organisation. The amount of support given by
other members of the organisation will rest largely on
the regard they have for the training department staff. So
any activity which heightens that regard will ultimately
benefit the training function.

3    An attempt to build an evaluation scheme into a training
programme often entails making some alterations and
additions to the original training framework. Our

experience has been that these modifications, irrespective of their evaluative purposes, regularly benefit the training in their own right. We shall have more to say about this in later chapters.

The book is set out in three parts. In the first part we outline some theoretical considerations which arise when training is to be evaluated. The major theme of this part of the book is that "evaluation" should be viewed more broadly than is commonly the case. Evaluation is not something which gets tagged on to the end of a training programme more or less as an afterthought. To be effective it needs to be carefully built into the programme, and systematic plans have to be worked out well before the training takes place.

So Part I opens with an account of a generalised framework for describing training evaluation. It moves on to examine the specific problems attached to the evaluation of supervisory and management training. The very nature of management jobs creates problems for the evaluator over and above those which are encountered in the evaluation of, say, operative or craft training. We believe that training administrators have been too ready to translate recommendations from operative training into the field of management training. A routine which is clearly suitable for operative training may be inappropriate when the trainees are managers. The relevance of this point to evaluation is discussed towards the end of Part I.

In Part II are presented thirteen case studies about the training of junior and middle managers. These are all evaluation projects with which we have been directly associated. They are described within the theoretical framework developed in Part I, but it is their practical implications which are stressed. Each of the case studies embodies features which are likely to be found in many training environments, and we hope that the project material in Part II will suggest practical applications in a wide variety of organisations.

Part III considers some of the more general issues raised by the need to evaluate training. It is stressed that there is no single evaluation question; of the several possible questions the training officer has to choose the one or more which are most appropriate in his case. It is argued that the questions which are most appropriate for management training are not necessarily those which are right in an operative training setting. And some doubt is cast on the practicality of advocating that training should always be evaluated.

Finally, some advice is given in the Appendix about the construction and use of questionnaires. Evaluation studies frequently involve the application of questionnaires which have to be constructed by a training officer himself. Many trainers have limited experience of questionnaire design, and the Appendix is intended to provide do-it-yourself hints which may guide some readers as they extend their evaluation efforts.

It is a pleasure to acknowledge our indebtedness to the Department of Employment and Productivity for the financial support which made possible the research described here.

# Part I

# A PRACTICAL FRAMEWORK FOR EVALUATING MANAGEMENT TRAINING

*Chapter I*

# The CIRO
# Framework of Evaluation

There are three fundamental questions which the trainer ought constantly to ask himself:

1    What needs to be changed?
2    What procedures are most likely to bring about this change?
3    What evidence is there that change has occurred?

The first two questions must be settled before any training can begin. The third, although it demands adequate consideration in advance, can be answered fully only after the training has been completed. It is the collection, assessment and effective use of information concerning these three questions which constitutes evaluation.

## 1:1    CONTEXT EVALUATION - WHAT NEEDS TO BE CHANGED?

No complex organisation can be perfect. There will be various reasons for the defects which are present, but in some cases they will be traceable to substandard performance on the part of someone in the organisation. The trainer needs to be aware of such situations either through his own investigations or by arranging that they are brought to his attention when they are discovered by others. He may be asked to advise on all cases where work performance is found to be inadequate, irrespective of its cause, but he is likely to be most concerned with those situations in which employees' current performance is regarded as falling short of their potential performance and where there are no obvious external constraints preventing an improvement. Once in possession of the relevant information the trainer will be in a position to decide on the training needs of the employees involved. During this process he can begin to consider the objectives he will set himself.

THREE LEVELS OF OBJECTIVES
It may be helpful if the trainer thinks in terms of objectives at three levels:

1    Ultimate objectives. The particular defect or defects in the organisation that he is hoping to eradicate
2    Intermediate objectives. The changes in employees' work behaviour that will be necessary if the ultimate objective is to be attained
3    Immediate objectives. The new knowledge, skills or attitudes that the employees must acquire before they will be capable of changing their behaviour in the required way

This three-way division of training objectives will reappear regularly throughout this book, since it is central to the evaluation framework which is being developed. It will be apparent that the three levels of objectives will not always be of equal relevance. However, for the present imagine a trainer who has collected information about a faulty work situation, who has assessed this information to establish training needs and who, on the basis of his findings, has set his training objectives. These processes will be collectively referred to as "context evaluation."

## 1:2   INPUT EVALUATION - WHAT PROCEDURES ARE MOST LIKELY TO BRING ABOUT CHANGE?

When the trainer has settled his objectives he must turn to a consideration of the resources he has at his disposal and consider how he can deploy them so as to maximise his chances of achieving his goals. Certain factors, such as the size of the departmental budget or the need to satisfy specific requirements of the industry's training board, may immediately limit the options open to him. But even with these particular constraints it is obvious that a trainer will always have a choice of actions.

If he is to make the most appropriate choice he will need certain information. Some of this he can obtain by drawing on his knowledge or past experience; some he will have to discover. Thus, when making his decision he will require information bearing on such points as: What are the relative merits of different training techniques? Is it feasible to run the training within the organisation or will the services of some external agency be needed? Does the age or background of the trainees suggest the inclusion or exclusion of any particular training method? How much time is likely to be available for training? What were the results last time a similar programme was run? These and other related questions will need to be answered at this stage. The processes of collecting evidence and using it to decide on the training procedures to be adopted will be referred to as "input evaluation."

## 1:3 OUTCOME EVALUATION – WHAT EVIDENCE IS THERE THAT CHANGE HAS OCCURRED?

This part of the training process – determining the extent to which training objectives have been achieved – is the one which is traditionally regarded as evaluation. Although the traditional, limited view of evaluation has been somewhat enlarged upon, it is because this aspect forms the major part of the process. It is concerned with the outcomes of training and therefore it will be referred to as "outcome evaluation."

## 1:4 THE FOUR STAGES OF OUTCOME EVALUATION

If outcome evaluation is to be successful it will require careful preparation well before the training programme begins; it will not be sufficient to ignore it until the training is actually under way. There are four stages which form part of any genuine attempt at outcome evaluation:

1    Defining training objectives
2    Selecting or constructing some measures of these objectives
3    Making the measurements at the appropriate time
4    Assessing the results and using them to improve later training

The first stage should have been accomplished as part of context evaluation. It is the second stage which is generally the greatest single obstacle to satisfactory outcome evaluation. As far as possible training objectives should be framed in a manner which will facilitate measurement. Easy to say, but much harder to achieve; in the last resort the problem of evaluation is a problem of measurement. Chapters 5 and 6 describe several methods of measuring the results of management training in the hope that these may furnish intending evaluators with some ideas on how to proceed. The Appendix provides more detailed information of a fundamental kind.

Decisions about the third stage of outcome evaluation – measuring at the appropriate time – will be influenced by the nature of the training objectives, and later in this book will be found the outline of a scheme that has been found helpful in this respect. However, at this point it must be mentioned that, in order to judge whether or not training has produced any changes, it is usually necessary to know what the situation was beforehand. In such cases measurement cannot wait until the completion of training but must be made before training is given as well as afterwards. This would obviously be impossible

B

if no thought were given to outcome until the end of training.

An outcome evaluation exercise would lose much of its point if the process ceased once the results had been collected. The results have no intrinsic importance of their own; they become valuable only if they are used as a means of improving the quality of later training. The primary purpose of gathering evaluation data is to provide the trainer with information that will help him increase his subsequent effectiveness. Thus in the fourth stage of outcome evaluation noted above the trainer assesses the evidence, draws his conclusions and uses them in the planning of future training.

## 1:5   THE THREE LEVELS OF OUTCOME EVALUATION

When investigating the results of training it has been found helpful to think in terms of a hierarchy of training outcomes. There are three levels in this hierarchy, corresponding to the three levels of training objectives introduced earlier in this chapter. These levels may conveniently be referred to in terms of immediate outcomes, intermediate outcomes and ultimate outcomes.

### LEVEL 1 - IMMEDIATE OUTCOMES
Successful training will produce some change in a trainee. Initially this training is reflected in alterations in his knowledge, skills or attitudes. Although these three are interrelated, it is often useful for the purposes of analysis to consider them separately. Changes in knowledge, skills or attitude can be measured as soon as a course has been completed, before a trainee leaves the training situation and in advance of his return to his job. These changes are the immediate outcomes of training.

### LEVEL 2 - INTERMEDIATE OUTCOMES

Training is not primarily concerned with learning for its own sake; its main concern is to bring about some positive change in the way a man does his job. The interest and importance of immediate outcomes (level 1) lie in the fact that they are in most cases necessary preliminaries to changes in the trainees' on-the-job behaviour (level 2) ; without such basic alterations at an immediate level there is little prospect of a change in job performance. But a change in knowledge, skill or attitude does not necessarily guarantee a change in job performance. There are many examples of training which fail to carry over into the work situation. To be successful, training must promote some changes in on-the-job behaviour. It is these changes which are the intermediate outcomes of training.

## LEVEL 3 - ULTIMATE OUTCOMES

If changes occur in the job behaviour of trainees then obviously
the organisation in which they work will be affected in some way.
For example, there may be alterations in departmental output,
costs, scrap rates, labour turnover or accident frequency. On
a more general plane the overall profitability or effectiveness of
the total organisation may be influenced. Changes of this nature
may be regarded as the ultimate outcomes of the training process.
They are not generally to be measured in terms of individual
behaviour (as the two previous levels are) but are indicated by
changes in an entire department or organisation. From the point
of view of the evaluator they present great difficulties. They
represent for the most part major departmental or organisational
objectives, so that many other members of the organisation over
and above the training staff will be working towards them. When
it happens that such objectives are attained it is hardly possible
to decide who, in particular, is responsible; the answer must be
that many people together contributed to their achievement. This
is why it is rarely practicable to evaluate specific training
programmes at this ultimate level. Attention throughout this book
will be mainly directed towards the earlier outcomes of training.

## 1:6   REACTION EVALUATION

So far in this chapter we have examined three aspects of evaluation.
"Context evaluation" has been defined in terms of the collection
and assessment of information about training objectives and needs.
"Input evaluation" has been viewed in terms of the processes of
collecting and using information to decide on training procedures.
Three levels of "outcome evaluation" have also been noted - in
terms of immediate outcomes, intermediate outcomes and ultimate
outcomes. One other aspect of evaluation needs to be introduced
before the scheme is complete; this is "reaction evaluation."

Reaction evaluation is defined in terms of the processes involved
in gaining and using information about trainees' expressed reactions.
Most trainers make some attempt to discover their trainees'
opinions of the course they have taken. This can be done in several
ways, both informal and formal - over-the-bar conversations, end-
of-course review sessions or follow-up inquiries about the
usefulness of the training experience. The distinguishing feature
of this type of evaluation is its reliance on the subjective reports

-19-

of trainees – their expressed reactions to the training. There is no doubt that trainees' views can prove extremely helpful and that this is especially so if care is taken to collect them systematically. Obtaining reaction evaluation material is generally a fairly straightforward matter, and several approaches will be discussed in later chapters.

1:7    CONCLUDING REMARKS

The four aspects of evaluation presented in this chapter may now be brought together as in Figure 1:1.

| EVALUATION TYPE | DEFINITION |
| --- | --- |
| Context evaluation | Obtaining and using information about the current operational context in order to determine training needs and objectives |
| Input evaluation | Obtaining and using information about possible training resources in order to choose between alternative "inputs" to training |
| Reaction evaluation | Obtaining and using information about trainees' expressed current or subsequent reactions in order to improve training |
| Outcome evaluation | Obtaining and using information about the outcomes of training in order to improve subsequent training. Three levels of outcome evaluation are in terms of immediate, intermediate and ultimate outcomes |

FIGURE 1:1    THE C I R O FRAMEWORK FOR THE EVALUATION
            OF TRAINING

The letters C I R O are the initials of context, input, reaction and outcome evaluation; outcome evaluation has three levels – concerned with immediate outcomes, intermediate outcomes and ultimate outcomes

It will be apparent that this scheme enlarges somewhat on the more usual conception of evaluation. It particularly emphasises the trainer's need for information. The fundamental purpose of acquiring this evaluation information is to help the trainer decide how he can best use his resources to increase the effectiveness of the training process and through this to make his contribution to the attainment of the organisation's objectives.

The practical aspects of these activities remain to be discussed, but two major questions have still to be broached. Should a training evaluator attempt all the C I R O activities described in Figure 1:1? And how does he set about the activities he does decide to attempt? The answers to these questions are dealt with in the following chapters.

# Chapter 2

# Specific Problems in the Evaluation of Management Training

"The effectiveness of training at managerial levels is difficult to assess and often impossible to measure." This quotation comes from a recent report of the Central Training Council ("Training and Development of Managers: Further Proposals," a report by the Management Training and Development Committee of the Central Training Council, HMSO, 1969) and aptly summarises the widely held view that training evaluation is particularly difficult when it involves management personnel. Part of the difficulty arises from the assumption that evaluation studies should be conducted at an intermediate outcome level - that training effectiveness should be assessed in terms of on-the-job changes in behaviour.

Such an assumption will be examined in this chapter. It will be argued that the practical problems it generates are very considerable, and that there are also good theoretical reasons why an emphasis solely on intermediate outcomes is an undesirable one.

## 2:1   VARIABILITY OF THE MANAGEMENT TASK

The practical problems involved in evaluating management training at an intermediate outcome level can be spotlighted by drawing attention to important differences between the jobs of managers and operatives. In the field of operative training it makes good sense to assess effectiveness in terms of on-the-job performance, but an uncritical extension of this into the management domain is much less sensible. Consider the clear differences between management and operative jobs.

### SHOP-FLOOR JOBS
In the case of many shop-floor jobs there tends to be a strictly limited number of ways in which they can be carried out successfully. A study of such jobs often enables one or two "best" ways of doing the

work to be identified, so that unsatisfactory work methods are fairly readily discovered. Training in these cases involves the learning of a set of correct procedures. The aim of the training is to eradicate the faults and to replace them with the approved methods of working. It is relatively easy to determine whether or not this has occurred: can or cannot the operative work at the acceptable standard?

## MANAGERIAL JOBS

With managerial work, however, there is much greater scope for individual approaches to a job. Given a similar set of objectives, different managers might choose to approach their task in quite different ways. Furthermore they might all be successful, for there is no single "correct" way of managing. It is, therefore, rarely possible to lay down hard and fast rules about the "best" form of managerial behaviour. And even when clearly inappropriate methods have been discovered their correction is not a matter of learning set procedures. Training is more likely to consist of the discussion of alternative approaches or the proposal of certain managerial guidelines. With this kind of training it is left to each trainee to attempt some integration of what he has learned, to decide what aspects of it are relevant to his own job, and then to apply it as he thinks fit. Thus the evaluator does not have the advantage of being able to watch for a specific change in a manager's behaviour, because the nature of the training process makes it impossible to predict exactly what form the change will take. Managerial training evaluation at an intermediate outcome level is obviously much more difficult than it is in the case of shop-floor trainees.

## REPETITION IN SHOP-FLOOR TASKS

A second crucial difference between management and operative work hinges on the fact that many shop-floor jobs involve the frequent repetition of a limited number of tasks. In an extreme form the worker might be continually performing a single operation, each cycle of which may last no longer than a minute. Related to this is the fact that criteria of satisfactory performance can often be stated in objective terms. It is these characteristics of shop-floor jobs which allow satisfactory assessments of worker effectiveness to be readily made. Thus, measuring the speed and accuracy of a machinist or typist can provide a fair estimate of their total work performance. And the measures are sufficiently precise to permit fine distinctions to be drawn between the abilities of individual workers.

## WIDE RANGE OF MANAGERS' DUTIES

In comparison, a managerial job is generally a compound of a wide range of separate tasks. Tasks may be repeated, but with some variation on each occasions; and the intervals between repetitions may be lengthy. The criteria of effective performance are frequently ill defined, subjective and of doubtful validity, so that it is impossible to gauge a manager's performance by one or two measures alone. And if the measurement criteria are suspect or can be set out only in broad terms (as is often the case), it becomes impossible to make accurate comparative judgements about the work of individual managers.

These practical differences between managers and operatives may be summarised in this way: manager's jobs are (a) much less tightly prescribed, and (b) much less regularly repeated and narrowly skilled than are operative jobs. Given this, the practicality may be questioned of always trying to assess the effectiveness of management training in terms only of changes at work. But there are other, more theoretical, reasons why intermediate outcome evaluation of management training is not always suitable.

## 2:2   FACTORS IN MANAGEMENT WORK BEHAVIOUR

In examining intermediate outcomes, it is necessary to look for changes in work behaviour brought about by a particular piece of training. This is fair enough if work behaviour is very largely determined by the training and hardly determined by any other factors. Such a situation often arises with operative training, but it is somewhat unusual in the case of managers.

Consider a manager at work some weeks after the training course which is now being evaluated. His work behaviour will be determined by many factors, of which these five are particularly important:

1   The success of the training at an immediate outcome level
2   The relevance of the training to the job
3   The leadership and organisational climate
4   His own personality and motivation
5   His subordinates

In Chapters 5 and 6 several of these factors will be examined in detail, but for now the following points will suffice.

## THE SUCCESS OF THE TRAINING AT AN IMMEDIATE OUTCOME LEVEL

There is no doubt that in the vast majority of cases job behaviour changes will occur only if the trainee has assimilated training material by the end of the course. A manager must have understood, say, network analysis or the company costing system by the end of his training if he is to be able to apply them readily when he returns to his job.

## THE RELEVANCE OF THE TRAINING TO THE JOB

It is fairly clear that unless training is relevant to a manager's job it will have no influence on his work behaviour. This aspect may be illustrated by the following brief account of one investigation carried out. In the course of a foreman-training programme instruction was provided about how to complete correctly the company's vacancy notification form. At the end of the training it was learnt that most foremen had retained this information (immediate outcome evaluation); later the completed forms submitted to the company employment office were examined (intermediate outcome evaluation). The required details were not being provided, and the piece of training was apparently a failure in terms of changes in work behaviour. But subsequent inquiries revealed that it was departmental managers rather than foremen who in practice completed the forms. The training had in fact been irrelevant.

## THE LEADERSHIP AND ORGANISATIONAL CLIMATE

The atmosphere between a manager and his colleagues is also a most important determinant of how he behaves. This will be examined further in Case Study K, but it is probably intuitively apparent that, unless a manager's boss and colleagues are concerned about new ideas and techniques, training him in these ideas and techniques will have little chance of on-the-job application. There have been instances, for example, where managers prevented their foremen from introducing the job descriptions advocated by the training department on the grounds that they might lead to inflexibility of working. And on other occasions foremen in a shift rota have been prevented from implementing changes in stock recording suggested during training because other foremen on the rota were opposed to them.

## IMPORTANCE OF PERSONALITY

A manager's own personality and motivation are also of clear importance. This aspect, however, is not always a training matter, and discussion will be postponed until Case Study K.

## INFLUENCE OF SUBORDINATES ON MANAGERS

The behaviour of a manager is often shown to have been influenced by those of whom he is in charge. It is interesting to note that shop-floor employees are in one sense more in control of their own effectiveness than are managers. It is often only machines which intervene between an operative and his work success, whereas for managers it is people. If these people are uncooperative or ineffective then the manager, too, may appear ineffective. A foreman taking part in an evaluation study had tried to develop a more participative style of supervision in line with what he had learned during training. Although he attempted to put this into effect, his subordinates were very reluctant to be drawn into a participative role, and the foreman was obliged to discontinue his experiment.

## 2:3 PRACTICAL RECOMMENDATIONS FOR TRAINING

Granted then that these five factors are important ones influencing how a manager behaves, the practical recommendations appear to be as set down in Figure 2:1.

| | FACTOR | | RECOMMENDATION |
|---|---|---|---|
| 1 | The success of the training at an immediate outcome level | 1 | Concentrate upon immediate outcome evaluation and improvement |
| 2 | The relevance of the training to the job | 2 | Concentrate upon context evaluation, emphasising training needs assessment |
| 3 | The leadership and organisational climate | 3 | Concentrate upon involving superiors and colleagues as part of a coherent training policy |
| 4 | His own personality and motivation | 4 | Concentrate upon motivational aspects of selection and training |

| 5 | His subordinates | 5 | Concentrate upon training at subordinate levels |

FIGURE 2:1 RECOMMENDATIONS AIMED AT CHANGING A MANAGER'S ON-THE-JOB BEHAVIOUR

It is tempting to argue on the basis of this table, that to ensure desirable intermediate outcomes of management training, steps should be taken to guarantee relevant training which is successful up to an immediate outcome level and which is part of an overall programme involving other departmental members. If this were done it might almost be possible to leave the intermediate outcomes to look after themselves - evaluation efforts could better be directed at the more practicable operations involved in context evaluation, input evaluation, reaction evaluation and immediate outcome evaluation.

For the practical and theoretical reasons outlined in this chapter, staff concerned with evaluation at the management training level could in many cases well direct their limited resources away from the intermediate outcomes of their training. Evaluation in terms of context, input, reaction and immediate outcomes is often likely to yield greater rewards.

One of these rewards has yet to be introduced. In Chapter 5 (Case Study F) the notion of a "self-correcting training system" will be examined. In this evaluation information is used to improve subsequent training. The idea is that it is necessary to get prompt and precise facts about the success of course number one in a series so that rapid modification can be made to the plans for course number two, three, four and so on. Such prompt and precise facts are often best gathered before the intermediate outcome level - before trainees have dispersed and the practical opportunities for evaluation are more limited.

2:4    SUMMARY

In summary, the themes of this chapter are two-fold: first that uncritical extension of operative training recommendations into the field of management training is to be avoided, and second that as far as management training evaluation is concerned it is often preferable for the practising training officer to concentrate on aspects other than training's immediate outcomes.

# Part 11

# CASE STUDIES

# Chapter 3

# Context Evaluation

This and the subsequent two chapters contain descriptions of thirteen actual evaluation exercises. They are presented as a series of case studies, and each study illustrates one or more of the types of evaluation set out in the CIRO framework of Chapter 1. This chapter describes two studies of context evaluation; Chapter 4 covers two studies of reaction evaluation; Chapter 5 contains accounts of six studies of immediate outcome evaluation; and Chapter 6 deals with three illustrations of intermediate outcome evaluation. None of the studies deals specifically with input evaluation, although this is touched upon several times. And, because of the enormous difficulty of attributing changes of the ultimate outcome kind to any one training programme, ultimate outcome evaluation is not discussed. In the final chapter, however, each aspect of evaluation will be discussed again and ultimate outcome evaluation will be further considered at that point.

For each of the thirteen case studies to be presented the background and aims are first spelled out. The method and summary results are then examined and discussed. It is hoped that this layout will suggest applications of the methods described to training specialists' own particular evaluation problems.

## 3:1 CONTEXT EVALUATION STUDIES

In Chapter 1 it was noted that part of the trainer's job is to take a close look at the current operational context of the organisation to determine which aspects of it might be improved by training, and in Chapter 2 it was pointed out that assessing the value of training is possible only if we know how relevant its aims are to the context in which it is carried out. This process of obtaining and using information about the operational situation has been termed "context evaluation." In practice it is to a large extent a question of determining the training needs of people in the organisation. Two studies, both aimed at establishing the training needs of supervisory personnel, will be described in this section.

BACKGROUND

One of the differences between operative and management training touched on in Chapter 3 lies in the greater difficulty attached to drawing up detailed job specifications for managerial positions. This has important implications for training needs identification as there is a strong body of opinion which advocates the determination of needs through a combination of job specification and individual appraisal.

The purpose of this first study was to see if there might be a viable shorter way of arriving at training needs. A complete account of this study is contained in a previous Training Information Paper (P B Warr and M W Bird, "Identifying Supervisory Training Needs," Training Information Paper 2, HMSO 1968) so the description here will be brief.

AIMS

The aims were twofold:

1    To investigate the possibilities of a problem-centred approach to training needs identification
2    To investigate individual differences in training needs

THE STUDY

Ninety-eight foremen were interviewed in detail about their work. These men had been selected to be broadly representative of the foremen employed in the iron and steel industry in the Sheffield region. One objective of the interview (the one to be examined here) was to learn which parts of each foreman's job gave rise to most of his difficulties. These were seen as areas of "exception" to the normal smooth running of his job.

By the time the interviews were completed a list had been collected of over 700 problems that the foremen had encountered. These problems were classified under ten separate headings. Thus all difficulties arising from lack of knowledge about machinery, personnel, procedures, and so on, were grouped together, as were problems centred upon the foreman's relations with his subordinates. This procedure of inquiring about and then classifying job difficulties allowed a detailed picture of a foreman's work problems to be quickly built up. From this information not only could individual training recommendations be made but it also became possible to predict to some extent the likely nature of the training needs of particular groups of foremen. For example, the frequency of job-knowledge problems and of difficulties springing from lack of confidence was particularly pronounced in the most recently appointed foremen. This was especially so amongst those who had no prior experience of acting in a supervisory capacity or who had taken over in a section in which they had not previously worked. This finding is not in itself surprising, but the obvious recommendation, that new supervisors should have intensive knowledge training about their particular job, is not always followed.

## COMMENTS
This investigation had a practical value as well as a theoretical interest, as it pointed to a possible way in which training staff can readily identify patterns of managerial training needs within their organisation. The "training-by-exception" procedure itself is relatively simple, yet in terms of results it can be as comprehensive as the detailed job specification and appraisal method.

### 3:3    Case B:   DIFFERING VIEWS ON SUPERVISORS' TRAINING NEEDS

## BACKGROUND
A chemical company was intending to make radical alterations to its work procedures, which would involve considerable reshaping of the jobs of the production and maintenance workers. Although the changes envisaged would primarily affect shop-floor personnel, the company recognised that these changes were such that the nature of supervisory jobs would also require some adjustment. Furthermore this was considered an opportune time both to enlarge supervisory jobs in certain respects and to make some alterations in the lower management structure of the organisation. The company therefore wanted to discover what changes were thought likely to occur in the jobs of its supervisors and to what extent they would need preparing for the different demands which their jobs would make on them in the future.

## AIMS
To survey opinions about:
1    The parts of the supervisors' jobs which were likely to be most affected by the proposed changes
2    The training the supervisors would require if they were to deal effectively with the new situation

## THE STUDY
Managers and supervisors from two separate production departments

c

were involved in this study. The proposed changes had been the subject of discussions amongst all grades of employees, and the people taking part in the investigation were very familiar with them. A list of twenty-eight supervisory activities and abilities was drawn up. These included such items as planning, selection and assessment, safety and liaison with other departments. Copies of this list were sent to all the production and maintenance managers and foremen in the two departments concerned. For each item on the list they were asked, individually:

1    To what extent they anticipated changes in this area of supervisory work

2    To what extent they believed training would be required in this area

Supervisors were asked to answer in respect of their own job and managers in respect of the jobs of the supervisors they controlled.

As expected, the areas where most change was foreseen were generally the areas in which most training was regarded as necessary. About some areas there was little difference of opinion amongst the people taking part in the study. Thus such topics as the training of subordinates and planning procedures came high on most people's lists for both change and training, whereas others, like familiarity with quality-control systems, were almost unanimously rated low on both counts.

However opinions were far from unanimous about certain of the items on the list. Managers and foremen often held different views, as did maintenance and production personnel and the members of the two departments. In the main there was agreement about those parts of supervisory work that would be most subject to change. But manager anticipated more changes than did foremen, and maintenance foremen expected greater alterations in their work then did their production colleagues.

Opinions were rather more divided about the items in which the supervisors would require training. For example an understanding of method-study techniques came close to the bottom of the foremen's list but was highly rated by the managers as a training priority. The opposite was the case where safety procedures were concerned. Production staff gave high priority to selection and assessment methods and low priority to a knowledge of trade union procedures, whereas the opinions of maintenance personnel on these two topics were the reverse of this. In the case of disciplinary functions, members of one of the departments gave it a high training-need rating although personnel of the other department saw it as being relatively unimportant.

## COMMENTS

This study and the previous one illustrate two points which will be well known to many training staff.

First, it would be totally misleading to assume that the training needs of all supervisors are more or less identical. Needs can differ along such lines as the type of work performed or the technology of the process with which the supervisor is concerned. Furthermore, the first study showed that training needs can also differ between supervisors doing virtually identical jobs but differing in their experience of the job, their age and their previous occupational background.

The second point of note from these studies is that views about the training requirements of particular supervisors may differ according to the source from which information is collected, so that it is not always easy for training staff to decide which set of opinions is most likely to be a true picture of the situation.

*Chapter 4*

# Reaction Evaluation

In this section are described two studies carried out at the reaction level. (Another, somewhat different, illustration of reaction evaluation is presented in Case N in Chapter 6.) As was described in Chapter 1, the aim in reaction evaluation is to obtain and use reliable information about trainees' expressed reactions to the training. In effect, the main concern here is about what trainees themselves think of the training, and the evaluator's problem is to develop measures which are easy to use and which give him detailed information so that he can modify the current or subsequent courses.

Experience has shown that trainees are very willing to assist in evaluation exercises providing that they can be reassured that it is the training rather than themselves that is being evaluated. If they are suspicious that the information they provide might be used for other purposes, such as checking on their abilities or in promotion reviews, then they are probably more likely to withhold their co-operation.

The first case in this chapter outlines a study in which the information collected was intended mainly for use in the planning of future training programmes. In the second study the information was analysed while the training continued, and the trainers used the results to help control the ongoing training process.

4:1   Case C :  THE COLLECTION OF TRAINEES' VIEWS ABOUT
               THE TRAINING PROGRAMME

BACKGROUND
A final review session is a common feature of most training programmes
In this the trainees have the chance of expressing their views on the course. The purpose of these sessions is generally to help the training staff to assess the success of their efforts and to provide them with information which may assist them when planning future programmes. Such sessions are, of course, a form of reaction evaluation, but in the way they are usually structured they tend to have several disadvantages. For example:

1      In the time available it is generally impossible to obtain the

views of all the trainees. So the opinions expressed may not be truly representative of the group as a whole

2      Social pressures may inhibit the expression of minority views

3      If training has lasted several days or perhaps weeks, trainees may have difficulty in recollecting details of the early parts of the programme

4      Trainees often disperse immediately after the review session. If they are keen to get away promptly this may mean that the session has to close prematurely

5      The form in which information is collected – long verbal reports – can make it hard to analyse and assess

In the type of training programme in which the content is divided up into a number of discrete sessions, the opinion was held that it would be possible to overcome most of the problems listed above. This could be done by using a standardised assessment form which is completed by the trainee shortly after the end of each session.

AIMS
To collect systematically trainees' views on specific aspects of their training.

THE STUDY
This study was spread over several training courses at both supervisory and management level. The courses were up to a fortnight in duration, and generally three or four separate sessions were scheduled for each day. At the end of each session every course member was asked to complete, independently, a "session assessment form." In this the trainee has three questions to consider at the conclusion of a session and he indicates his answer by putting a mark in what is for him the appropriate interval in each scale. An illustration of a session assessment form is shown in Figure 4:1.

For scoring purposes the intervals along each scale were numbered from 1 to 7 starting from the unfavourable (left), so that a high number indicated a favourable reaction. At the conclusion of a course the evaluator totalled the marks given to each session by every trainee. This was of course done separately for enjoyment, information and relevance. The total session marks were then divided by the number of trainees, so giving average session scores. It was also found helpful to rank the sessions in order – for example, from most to least enjoyable – as this made it

1    Enjoyment of session

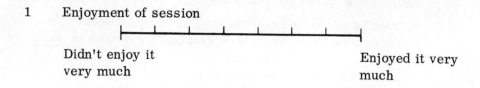

   Didn't enjoy it                        Enjoyed it very
   very much                              much


2    Amount of new information picked up during session

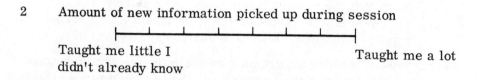

   Taught me little I                     Taught me a lot
   didn't already know


3    Relevance of session to own job

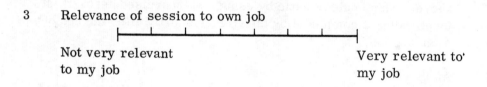

   Not very relevant                      Very relevant to'
   to my job                              my job


FIGURE 4:1  SESSION ASSESSMENT FORM


easier to develop a rapid overall appraisal of the total programme.
The results from such a reaction evaluation study are shown in
Figure 4:2.

If the evaluator wished to use this information to help him in
the planning of future programmes he would quickly notice the
results of the Manpower Planning session. Here was a topic which
was highly relevant to the work of the trainees, but not only had they
found it relatively unenjoyable but, what is perhaps more important,
it had also apparently added little to what they already knew about
the subject. Obviously the trainer would wish to remedy this in
subsequent courses.

If the evaluator has the time he may find it helpful to go more
deeply into the session assessment information. It is often possible
to take the assessments of particular groups of trainees and analyse
them separately. For example, in the course illustrated in Figure 4:2
trainees came from several companies of various sizes. The
assessments made by trainees from small firms were compared with
those made by members of large companies. It then came to light

that the Industrial Relations and Negotiating Exercise sessions were rated as very relevant by the personnel from larger firms, but much less so by the trainees from smaller firms. Possibly the degree of unionisation amongst the workpeople was not so high in the smaller as it was in the larger companies represented, so that managers from these firms had less concern with formal industrial relations procedures. But whatever the reason may have been, it did indicate that the training needs of the two groups of managers were being provided for with differential success.

It was also sometimes found informative to analyse reaction on the basis of the type of work the trainees performed. On a series of internal company courses various differences were found between the assessments of line and of staff supervisors. These were most pronounced in the relevance ratings of sessions.

By combining the results from several similar courses it became possible to compare trainees' reactions to participation sessions (for example, case studies, projects, visits) and non-participation sessions (for example, lectures, films). It was found, for instance, that assessments of the two types of session tended to be similar when they took place in the morning, but that non-participation sessions were in general assessed much less favourably than others when they occurred in the afternoon. This supports the view, widely held by training staff, that in after-lunch sessions it is better that trainees should be actively involved rather than passively listening. A further finding about these two types of session which may be of interest was that younger trainees gave more favourable enjoyment ratings to participation sessions than did their older colleagues.


COMMENTS

More details about the use of session assessment forms are given in the Appendix. There are, however, several points relating to this form of reaction evaluation which are worth mentioning:

1    The questions on the form illustrated above ask how enjoyable, how informative, and how relevant a session was. Obviously there are other features of a session about which the evaluator might want information. For example trainees' views on the length of the session, the amount of time available for discussion, or the level of presentation might be required. If so, appropriate questions can easily be framed

2    A disadvantage of all standardised forms is that they limit the information the evaluator can obtain to that which is

| TITLE OF SESSION | Enjoyment | Information | Relevance |
|---|---|---|---|
| Setting Management Objectives | 12 | 10 | 7 |
| Organisation Structure | 3 | 5 | 6 |
| The Industry Today | 10 | 11 | 14 |
| The Company and its Environment | 1= | 2 | 12 |
| Communication Systems | 7 | 13 | 4 |
| Accident Prevention | 4 | 6 | 1 |
| Industrial Relations | 5= | 3 | 8= |
| Negotiating Exercise | 1= | 1 | 10 |
| Technical Developments | 13 | 12 | 13 |
| Control Techniques | 5= | 4 | 11 |
| Manpower Planning | 14 | 14 | 5 |
| Business Game | 8= | 7= | 8= |
| Accident Prevention Project | 11 | 9 | 2 |
| Training | 8= | 7= | 3 |

FIGURE 4:2   COURSE MEMBERS' ASSESSMENT OF SESSIONS

## AVERAGE SCORE
(best possible = 7, worst possible = 1)

| Enjoyment | Information | Relevance |
| --- | --- | --- |
| 4.9 | 4.6 | 5.1 |
| 6.3 | 5.3 | 5.6 |
| 5.5 | 4.4 | 2.9 |
| 6.5 | 5.8 | 4.3 |
| 5.7 | 4.1 | 6.0 |
| 6.0 | 4.9 | 6.8 |
| 5.9 | 5.7 | 5.0 |
| 6.5 | 5.9 | 4.9 |
| 4.7 | 4.3 | 3.1 |
| 5.9 | 5.5 | 4.5 |
| 4.5 | 3.6 | 5.8 |
| 5.6 | 4.8 | 5.0 |
| 5.4 | 4.7 | 6.3 |
| 5.6 | 4.8 | 6.2 |

contained in the questions he actually asks. He can of course partially overcome this by putting an "other comments" section at the bottom of the form, and this is a procedure which may be found helpful

3       In the studies described above, the analysis of session assessments was left until the end of the training programme. The evaluator can, however, collect and examine assessment immediately after each session. This procedure has two advantages. First it gives the evaluator a chance to make inquiries about any unusual ratings before the trainees disperse. Second it may allow him to correct, within the duration of the present course, any deficiencies that the assessments may have brought to light.

4:2     Case D : MONITORING MANAGEMENT GAMES

BACKGROUND
In some circumstances it may be important to obtain information about training while it is actually in progress. A typical situation arises in the use of open-ended business games (games which can be continued for an indefinate number of moves), where the trainer may be unsure of the optimum time at which to terminate the game. If he terminates too soon, then he has wasted a potential learning experience, if he terminates too late he risks frustration and boredom from the players. He therefore needs some method of monitoring players' reactions, so that he has information which will help him to decide the best point at which to finish the game. Even experienced game users find it difficult to assess how players are reacting to the game, particularly where the participants may be scattered about in different rooms. Experience gained from previous runs of the same game does not serve as a very good guide to future runs because the games may often progress at different speeds, so that the optimum termination point last time the game was played will act only as a very rough guide to termination on future runs.

AIMS
To give trainers some simple monitoring information enabling them to decide when to terminate an open-ended management game.

THE STUDIES
Several management and business games have been examined using forms similar to that illustrated in the previous study. The only difference lay in the addition of a fourth scale which measured

opinions about the length of each gaming session. So the forms, when . completed, provided running information on players' perceptions of enjoyment, learning, relevance and duration of each gaming session or period. After each session the completed forms were returned to the game controller, where they were immediately added up and averaged in the way described in the previous study. The averages were then plotted on graphs to show how ratings on each scale were changed from session to session. Figure 4:3 shows a typical graph for players' ratings of learning during the course of the game.

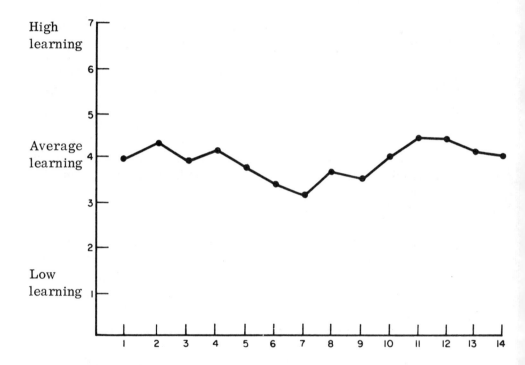

FIGURE 4:3 AVERAGE REACTION ON THE SCALE ASSESSING
JUDGED AMOUNT OF LEARNING IN A SESSION

Notice that there are two peaks to this graph, one early on in the game and one which occurs much later. This is quite a frequent finding, and from interviews with players it seems that the first peak occurs where players are learning the rules and mechanics of the game. The later peak results from the learning of strategies which enable players to establish some control over these rules. The trainer is concerned mainly with this second peak because he is normally interested only in the mechanics of a game as a means to the learning of its strategies.

In the example, ratings for learning, as shown in Figure 4:3, were tailing off after session 13. Enjoyment ratings (not shown here) had been stable since session 10; relevance ratings were just beginning to tail off, while ratings of whether there was enough time allocated to the session had shown since session 11 that players felt too much time was available. In the light of this information, the game controller decided to terminate the game at session 14.

## A FURTHER STUDY

Another study with management games provides some confirmatory evidence that the best time to terminate a game is when the average learning rating is just past its maximum. Thirty-two people, in groups of 4, were playing a resources-utilisation game. After 12 sessions, when the learning ratings began to fall off, 4 of the 8 groups stopped playing. The other 4 groups continued for 6 more sessions. All players then filled in a questionnaire to discover what they had learned about the strategies of the game. There was no significant difference between the learning of those whose game was terminated after session 12 and those who had experienced the 50 per cent playing time up to session 18.

## ADDITIONAL SOURCES OF INFORMATION

Although in these studies players' ratings for learning were used as the primary basis for deciding when to stop the game, enjoyment, job relevance and duration ratings all provided useful information. Ratings for job relevance tended to show very little variation during the course of a game, except where the game included a number of exercises, problems of sub-games which made individual sessions particularly relevant to the job problems of certain players. Enjoyment ratings tended to be low in the early stages of a game while players struggled with the laborious business of learning the rules. Otherwise they followed a similar pattern to the ratings for learning, except in sessions where perceived enjoyment fell off badly as the result of a disastrous gaming decision.

## COMMENTS

The most useful scale for manipulating the game while it is in progress is the rating for session duration. If a player or group of players indicates that there was far too little time available for early sessions, it may well be a sign of difficulty in learning the rules of the game. It may be necessary to extend the time limit on these early sessions to ensure that the rules are properly understood. Conversely, judgements that too much time was available, when they occur frequently, are an indication that the game is getting too easy and are usually associated with a fall-off in players' perceptions of learning.

The use of session assessment forms as a means of monitoring the progress of a particular type of management game does not exhaust their potential usefulness in reaction evaluation. Where games are not divided up into discrete decision periods but run continuously, control information can be acquired by asking players to complete assessment forms at predetermined time intervals. And their use need not be confined to gaming exercises. With suitable modifications, either of form design or of procedures, they can be employed in other training situations in which trainees engage in one kind of activity over a period of time. Thus the progress of a case study committee, the headway made with a structured task or the developments within a sensitivity training group are all activities which might be monitored by variations on the basic method described in this study.

*Chapter 5*

# Immediate Outcome Evaluation

The studies of reaction evaluation presented in the last chapter have in common a reliance on what trainees say. They employ, for example, measures of how much trainees say that they have learned. Whereas there are many situations in which this kind of information is valuable, it will often be preferable to develop objective measures of how much they actually have learned. (Reaction information can, of course, also be gathered in these latter cases.)

When measures of actual learning are being looked for (rather than assumed learning as is measured in reaction evaluation), then outcome evaluation must be brought into the picture. In this chapter are described six studies of the immediate outcomes of management training - the changes immediately consequent upon a training programme. These studies are categorised in terms of changes in knowledge (three examples), changes in skill (two examples) and changes in attitude (one example). Such a classification is of course valid only in principle; in practice the three types of training effects may be closely intertwined.

## 5:1   CHANGES IN KNOWLEDGE

A large proportion of the bread-and-butter work of a training department involves transmission of factual material to supervisors and managers. In these common situations, where the knowledge to be imparted is fairly clearly defined, the measurement of immediate training outcomes is relatively straightforward.

## 5:2   Case E  : IMPROVEMENT IN KNOWLEDGE DURING SUPERVISORY COURSES

BACKGROUND
The first study in this group deals with the general issues involved in such a project. In order to acquire information about the immediate success of training the trainer must have some measure of the trainees' pre- and post-training knowledge levels. The work described here was carried out to discover how feasible it was to obtain such measures, as well as to look into certain other factors which

might influence the immediate outcome of typical knowledge-based programmes.

AIMS

The two aims in this case were:

1 To measure knowledge improvement during supervisory training
2 To examine factors which might be important in determining the extent of knowledge gain

THE STUDY

The method used was a questionnaire completed by the trainees both before and after their training. The "pre-test" was given immediately before the commencement and the "post-test" as soon after the end of the training as possible, usually before the trainees dispersed. The pre-test and post-test questionnaires were identical, and the evaluation to be discussed was solely in terms of the factual content of the training programme. Questionnaire items which would have needed long written answers were avoided. A questionnaire contained about twenty-five items and took a maximum of half an hour for a trainee to complete.

Four separate programmes run by a large steel group were studied. They were all residential courses of up to five days' duration. Their primary purpose was to give certain factual information to newly appointed foremen. The firm appointed about forty-five such foremen each year; and since this was too large a number to be handled conveniently on a single training course, each of the four programmes was put on three times a year with about fifteen trainees attending on each occasion. This system proved an advantage as attendance could be made at the first course of each series of three as observers. This experience afforded an opportunity for a course questionnaire to be drawn up for examining the remaining two courses in that series.

The general pattern of results is set out in Figure 5:1 in which the titles of the four programmes are listed in the left column.

The average pre-test scores for all programmes were around the 50 per cent mark showing that some of the information was already known to some trainees. On average the post-test scores of all four programmes were 20 per cent up on pre-test results.

An item-by-item analysis of the pre-test results showed which material was initially known to most trainees and also which items the majority of trainees were unable to answer. This information

PERCENTAGE SCORE

| NAME OF PROGRAMME | NUMBER OF TRAINEES TESTED | Pre-test | Post-test | Improvement |
|---|---|---|---|---|
| 1 Company Information | 30 | 52.0 | 71.1 | 19.1 |
| 2 Industrial Relations | 30 | 50.4 | 74.2 | 23.8 |
| 3 Training and Interview Techniques | 28 | 49.2 | 68.2 | 19.0 |
| 4 Accident Prevention | 31 | 50.2 | 74.3 | 24.1 |

FIGURE 5:1  IMPROVEMENT IN KNOWLEDGE FOLLOWING
SUPERVISORY TRAINING

helped training staff decide which topics to retain and which to discard on future programmes. Using the post-test results as well, the items on which most trainees had improved in knowledge were discovered. Similarly the areas where least improvement had occurred were located, allowing a distinction to be made as to which areas of the training needed to be reviewed before the next similar course began. This topic is considered further in the following study.

In this investigation there was the additional aim of discovering if the knowledge of each of the foremen undergoing training improved by a roughly equivalent amount. So the results of different groups of trainees were compared with one another. Comparisons were made on the basis of the type of department in which the foremen worked, their age, their educational background and their intelligence. This last was known because the firm concerned used intelligence tests as part of their selection procedure for supervisory staff. The results of these comparisons are given in Figure 5:2. Details are given for only one of the four training programmes but the results in the other three were essentially similar.

There was little difference in either pre- or post-test scores between production and non-production personnel, so this particular variable did not seem to influence training effectiveness. However,

| NAME OF GROUP | NUMBER OF PEOPLE IN GROUP | PERCENTAGE SCORE | | |
|---|---|---|---|---|
| | | Pre-test | Post-test | Improvement |
| All trainees | 30 | 50.4 | 74.2 | 23.8 |
| Production trainees | 16 | 50.4 | 72.7 | 22.3 |
| Non-production trainees | 14 | 50.4 | 75.9 | 25.5 |
| Trainees aged 37 and under | 15 | 46.6 | 77.8 | 31.2 |
| Trainees aged over 37 | 15 | 54.2 | 70.5 | 16.3 |
| Trainees educated at grammar school | 14 | 49.4 | 79.0 | 29.6 |
| Trainees educated at secondary modern school | 16 | 51.3 | 70.0 | 18.7 |
| Best 12 performers on intelligence tests | 12 | 52.2 | 79.4 | 27.2 |
| Remainder of intelligence-tested foremen | 13 | 47.7 | 67.4 | 19.7 |

FIGURE 5:2  FURTHER ANALYSIS OF THE INDUSTRIAL RELATIONS PROGRAMME

when the results were examined on the basis of the trainees' age, the older foremen were found to do better on the pre-test than their younger colleagues. This was presumably because of their greater experience of the course topics. But their post-test scores, and hence their improvement scores, were considerably lower than those of the younger foremen. This suggests, as do the results of other research, that typical knowledge-based training procedures are more suited to younger people than to older trainees who may long since have lost their "classroom skills."

The results from the analysis by education and by intelligence can be discussed together. Despite similar pre-test scores, there are clear differences in post-test scores. The more intelligent

D

foremen, and those who had received grammar-school-level education (two obviously overlapping categories) acquired factual knowledge during the training to a greater extent than did the other foremen. These differences, as well as those between older and younger foremen were statistically very significant.

COMMENTS

The association between a supervisor's age, intelligence and educational background and his ability to learn factual material during training is of more than theoretical importance. It raises several practical questions. For example, is there a case for providing separate training facilities for older foremen? If this were done it would give the trainer scope to use techniques more suited to older trainees. More time could perhaps be scheduled for their training to compensate for their slower rate of learning. Or would such a segregation lose the advantage of having a mixture of youth and experience on the same programme? Would trainees resent being streamed in this way? There are unfortunately far more questions than answers at present. However, if the trainer is not only aware that wide differences in learning ability exist but also has a few guidelines to help him predict who the "good" and "bad" learners will be, he can make appropriate provisions when designing his programmes. In the present case the immediate outcome evaluation information was used to modify subsequent courses - a procedure which is developed in the next case.

For now, it may be noted that the method outlined here is appropriate for the immediate level evaluation of most knowledge-based training. The chief requirement is a suitable questionnaire for measuring the trainees' knowledge on a before-and-after basis. It is not claimed that designing knowledge-testing questionnaires is a simple task, but with a little practice it is well within the capabilities of training staff. And the amount of evaluation information that they produce often justifies the time spent on constructing them. (There are other advantages too; see Case G.) There have been several cases of training officers who evaluate their programmes using questionnaires they have developed themselves. Advice on question-naire design which may help other evaluators is given in the Appendix.

5:3    Case F : A SELF-CORRECTING TRAINING SYSTEM

BACKGROUND

It has already been suggested several times that the purpose of evaluation studies is to provide information which permits training to be improved. This information (see Chapter 1) can be of several kinds, but in the previous case study attention was drawn to the analysis of knowledge questionnaires serving as pre- and post-tests. By examining areas where training is seen from the questionnaires to be relatively unsuccessful, focused changes can be introduced which are likely to improve later courses.

Carrying out this getting-and-using-information procedure in a systematic fashion can be viewed as establishing a "self-correcting training system" - one which corrects itself. In theory, as the evaluation information enables the trainer to detect areas where changes are needed and gives him feedback on the success or failure of any changes which he makes, a series of courses evaluated in this way should show a continuing increase in training effectiveness.

But it could be argued that any continuing series of courses would improve, whether evaluation measures were used or not, because trainers are quite able to detect areas of the course which could be made more effective without the need for complex evaluation measures. In order to assess whether systematic feedback from evaluation has any advantage over the informal feedback which a trainer receives from his own observations, this next study compares two series of courses, one using evaluation measures and one relying on the observations and intuitions of the trainers.

## AIM
To assess the effectiveness of a self-correcting training system, compared with the usual method of improving courses from informal observations.

## THE STUDY
Two series of similar information-giving courses in an airline were chosen for this study. In each case the following procedure was used. Speakers on both series of courses were interviewed and asked what they hoped course members would know after their session which they did not know before it. Speakers' replies formed the basis of a knowledge questionnaire which was answered by course members at the beginning and the end of each course. In addition, ratings for enjoyment, information, relevance and duration of session were completed by course members at the end of each session, using the reaction evaluation technique described in Studies C and D and in the Appendix. So, at the end of the course, information was available to show how much of the contents of each session course members knew before it started, how much they knew at the end of the course, how much they enjoyed each session, how relevant they thought it to their

work, and whether they felt that too much or too little time was available for the session.

COMPARISONS BETWEEN THE TWO SERIES
In the first series of courses, Series A (the terms "first" and "second" are used for descriptive convenience; in practice both series were running concurrently), although these measures were taken, the results were not revealed to the trainers. This meant that any improvements in course design were made in the absence of systematic evaluation information. In contrast, for the second series (Series B), the results were given to the training staff and incorporated into plans for improving subsequent runs. Taking the average knowledge improvement (post-test minus pre-test) on the first course in each series as a base line, it was possible to examine how the two courses improved with repetition.

Percentage improvement
beyond the first course
in each series

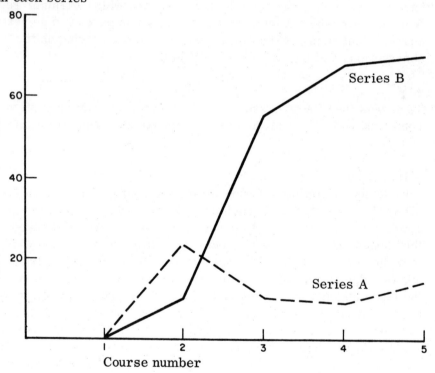

FIGURE 5:3  COMPARISON OF COURSE SERIES WITH AND
            WITHOUT FEEDBACK

As Figure 5:3 shows, the improvement after five courses for the series without feedback information was some 10 per cent above the level of the first course. However, for the series of courses with feedback from evaluation, the equivalent improvement was 70 per cent. This clearly demonstrates the greater effectiveness of systematic feedback in bringing about improvements in a series of courses compared with traditional methods relying solely on the informal observations of the trainer.

COMMENTS

In many companies the "bread-and-butter" work of the training department is to run routine courses which are repeated whenever the need arises. Such courses are always in danger of "solidifying," so that their content and organisation ceases to be questioned. It is these courses which are particularly likely to gain from the self-correcting system approach. As this study has shown, the improvements (here measured in terms of knowledge gain) can be very considerable.

Yet other types of improvement can follow from the adoption of this approach. Repeated use of course feedback can lead to the elimination of redundant sessions, other sessions being abbreviated, and to a general tightening up of standards, As this happens the training department may well find that a five-day course can be cut to one of four days. Such a saving can be readily expressed in financial terms, and it may perhaps be backed up by evidence from subsequent evaluation studies that trainees' knowledge-gain in four days is equivalent to that previously achieved in a full working week. Such a state of affairs would clearly be very satisfactory.

5:4 Case G: THE EFFECTS OF PRE-TEST QUESTIONNAIRES
ON LEARNING

BACKGROUND

Each of the two previous studies used questionnaires to assess changes in knowledge. The process of compiling a knowledge questionnaire can be demanding, and the training pay-off of such measures deserves to be closely examined. One valuable form of pay-off has been stressed in the previous study; now a different kind of benefit should be discussed. If, before training begins, a trainee is asked a number of questions on the key issues to be covered during the programme, then he might be expected to pay particular attention when these topics came up during the training. And if the trainee is told that he will be questioned again on these same topics at the end of training, then

a pre-course questionnaire would not only be likely to alert him
to the key issues when they arose but might also lead him to remember
them as well.

AIM
To discover whether questionnaires are in themselves useful training
devices.

THE STUDIES
These investigations were carried out during a series of accident-
prevention courses arranged for supervisors in a steel firm.
Supervisors who were about to attend one of the courses were divided
into two groups. The members of these two groups were matched for
age, intelligence and educational background. One group, the
"experimental" group, was given a pre-course questionnaire which
covered some of the factual material that would be presented during
training. The other, the "control" group, was not asked to answer a
questionnaire before training. Apart from this original difference, the
two groups were treated identically on the same course.

DIFFERENTIAL PERCENTAGE IMPROVEMENTS
After the course, as a post-test, trainees in both groups answered
the questionnaire. By assuming that the average pre-test score of
the control group would be roughly similar to that of the experimental
group with which it had been matched, it was possible to calculate
percentage improvements for both groups. The control group (that
is, the one without the pre-course questionnaire) improved on average
by 35 per cent. The experimental group (the one which had answered
the pre-course questionnaire) showed an average improvement of
66 per cent over their pre-test level. This difference between the
two groups was statistically highly significant, despite the fact that
they had both attended the same course. So a pre-course questionnaire can be a most helpful training aid: by including questions on
key facts in a pre-test, the training officer can increase the chances
of the trainees' being able to remember these facts at the end of
the programme.

THE VALUE OF A PRE-COURSE QUESTIONNAIRE
Many training officers accept these results but fear that by
alerting trainees to specific issues at the outset there is a danger
of making them disregard other important topics in the programme.
A further study has been carried out which shows that this is not so:
instead of decreasing the amount of non-questionnaire material learned,

the use of a pre-course questionnaire may actually increase the learning of this material.

For this second study two quite different pre-test questionnaires, both on accident-prevention topics, were prepared. A post-test was formed by putting together all the questions in the two pre-tests into a single questionnaire. This time the trainees were split into three matched groups. One of these, the control group, again had no pre-test. The foremen in the two experimental groups were each given one or other of the two pre-tests. All trainees attempted the post-test, (made up of the combined pre-tests) at the end of the training. The members of the control group had seen none of the post-test questions before while the members of the experimental groups had all seen half of the post-test questions before. The results were as in Figure 5:4

| GROUP | | IMPROVEMENT |
|---|---|---|
| Control group (without pre-test) | | 37% |
| Experimental groups (with pre-test) | | |
| 1 | On questions not previously asked | 51% |
| 2 | On questions asked as pre-test | 65% |

FIGURE 5:4  IMPROVEMENT ON PRE-COURSE SCORES OF THREE GROUPS OF FOREMEN

COMPARISONS TO BE DRAWN

Two separate comparisons need to be made here. First the 37 per cent improvement of the control group with the 65 per cent improvement of the experimental groups on questions they had seen as a pre-test. This difference makes the same point as did the study described previously: people retain more material (as shown in post-test scores) if they have been alerted to these questions through a pre-test.

Second the control group's 37 per cent improvement with the experimental groups' 51 per cent improvement. Since none of the items in this comparison had been seen previously, there is no reason to expect one group to be better than the other. Yet the experimental groups are significantly better on these new items in the post-test. It must be concluded that the pre-course questionnaire may actually improve course members' retention of material which was not covered by pre-test questions.

## COMMENTS

The use of a pre-test may improve course members' learning of factual material in two ways: by alerting people to specific questions and motivating them to remember those questions; and by assisting in organising other related material so that it is more easily remembered. It is necessary to add a caution on the second, generalised, function of the pre-test questionnaire. Obviously a questionnaire is unlikely to help the course member to remember material which is not in some way related to the contents of the questionnaire. So a questionnaire on Spanish history would be unlikely to help in the retention of material on accident prevention. But where questionnaire and training material are related, as in the accident-prevention course studied, a pre-test made up of a limited number of representative items drawn from the course content should, in itself, bring about a general improvement in course members' learning of factual material.

## QUESTIONNAIRES IMPROVE PRESENTATION

There is a further advantages that questionnaires possess. When a training officer who is drawing up the questionnaire is obliged to review his own grasp of a subject, he is very likely to improve his subsequent presentation of it during the actual training. This virtue of questionnaire construction is of course even more apparent when outside speakers are being asked to provide their own criterion questions; clear improvements in delivery and organisation have regularly been observed when outside speakers have preceded their talk by considering the aims they wish to embody in a questionnaire.

## RETENTION OF KNOWLEDGE

Finally a question which is relevant to all evaluation of knowledge based training - for how long will trainees retain the knowledge they have acquired? The answer must depend upon how often they are called upon to use that knowledge in their work (see also the discussion in Chapter 2, summarised in Figure 2:1). If they use it regularly, they are likely to remember it indefinitely, but if the knowledge is rarely required it is likely, sooner or later, to be forgotten. How soon will depend upon individual cases, but a simple extension of the basic method used in the last three case studies can supply the answer. By asking trainees to complete the questionnaire a third time, say six months after the training, the evaluator can discover how much of the knowledge initially learned has been retained.

## 5:5   CHANGES IN SKILL

The previous three studies have examined training with a primarily
factual content.  An examination should now be made of the immediate
outcome evaluation of skills training – an activity which is often thought
to defy evaluation.  If "evaluation" is taken to mean intermediate or
ultimate outcome evaluation, the difficulties are indeed formidable.
But, as argued in Chapter 2, it is assessment up to the immediate
outcome level which is often particularly appropriate for management
training, and here the measurement difficulties are not so severe.

The most practicable procedures involve ratings of some kind by
the trainer or by other observers.  A trainer who has specified his
objectives in advance will often be able to set up some sort of rating
scales to describe the behaviour he is dealing with.  By systematically
recording his judgements about trainees' behaviour he can adequately
assess the effectiveness of training.  The two studies in this section
provide illustrations of this point;  they may perhaps provide some
ideas for trainers to adapt for their own situation.

## 5:6   Case H : LEARNING AN INTERVIEWING SKILL

### BACKGROUND
As part of its supervisory training programme a company gave more
than a day's training time to interviewing techniques with particular
emphasis on the selection or employment interview.  Initially trainees
were given verbal instruction in interview procedures.  This included
a session on the principles that should govern the conduct of interviews,
followed by an account (based on the National Institute of Industrial
Psychology's Seven-Point Plan) of the type of information that should
be sought during an employment interview.  Trainees then watched
a simulated interview between two members of the training staff.
After a short interval to allow them to prepare notes and so on, each
trainee was asked to carry out a selection-type interview.

### AIM
To discover the effectiveness of the trainees' interviews.

### THE STUDY
For the practical interview sessions, trainees were divided into
groups of four members.  Thirty-two trainees were involved in all,
so there were eight such groups.  Each member of the group in
turn carried out an interview, while the other three members of his
group and a member of the training staff studied his performance

from the background. Each trainee in a group interviewed a different subject. The subjects were all young members of the company with whom the trainees had had no previous contact.

At the end of each interview the other three members of the group and the trainer commented on the way the interview had been carried out, both in terms of its conduct and the amount, quality and relevance of the information that had been obtained from the subject. There were also suggestions about how the interview could have been improved.

The trainee who carried out the first interview in each group of four had no opportunity to watch and criticise the performance of his colleagues, so that his interview preparation was based mainly on the largely theoretical instruction he had received. Later interviewers in the group had had the chance of observing the efforts of at least one of their colleagues.


METHOD OF ASSESSMENT
An assessment of the interviewers' performance was made by the member of the training staff who sat in with each group of trainees. Assessments were made on a standardised form, in terms of:

1      Information collected. A list of seventeen topics, drawn from the Seven-Point Plan, was drawn up. An interviewer was awarded a mark for each topic that he had touched upon and a further mark if he covered the topic in some depth. The maximum possible information score was thus thirty-four

2      Technique. This was a record of the mistakes made during the interview and included such items as the number of occasions on which the interviewer had asked a leading question, got off the point or interrupted the subject's answers

The information scores are summarised in Figure 5:5. It is apparent from this table that later interviewers were obtaining, on average, more information about their subjects than were those who had preceded them. Further analysis showed that the higher scores of later interviewers were not so much because of their inclusion of more topics as because they covered topics in more detail.

However, where interviewing technique was concerned there was no evidence of any falling off in the number of mistakes made during an interview. The final interviewers made as many errors of techniqu as had the trainees who had performed first. The two most frequent mistakes were asking leading questions and failing to follow up promising leads, each of which occurred at least once during approximately two-thirds of the interviews.

Finally it is interesting to note, that, unlike the knowledge-gain results described in Case E, the trainees' scores were not related to their age, educational background or intelligence.

| Position of interview in group | 1st | 2nd | 3rd | 4th |
|---|---|---|---|---|
| Number of interviewers involved | 8 | 8 | 8 | 8 |
| Average information score | 11.3 | 12.9 | 15.7 | 16.4 |

FIGURE 5:5  INFORMATION ELICITED BY DIFFERENT GROUPS
OF INTERVIEWERS


COMMENTS

Very few skills can be effectively acquired solely by listening to theoretical descriptions of how to perform them. Some form of practice or participation is needed if the best use is to be made of training time. Ideally the trainee would be given several chances to practise the skill personally. But if time does not permit this then the opportunity of watching and criticising his colleagues' efforts can lead to an improvement in the trainee's performance. Obviously this would not apply to all types of skills, but if the skill is of an appropriate type, as for example in job instruction, negotiating and committee procedures, then the observe-and-comment method can be a useful technique.

In the present study a fairly straightforward procedure for evaluating trainees' performance was developed. Similar methods can be applied to many skills-training situations when immediate-outcome information is required. Granted that the trainer has specified his objectives in a clear-cut way, then there is often no real difficulty attached to the appraisal of skilled performance in the training situation; subjective but systematic assessment by qualified trainers is a perfectly satisfactory procedure. The practical problem which might arise is that time is apparently not available to put each trainee in turn "through his paces." Yet, as this study has shown, such an operation has clear training value in addition to the built-in evaluation benefits it carries. In this case, as in many others, training and evaluation functions are closely intertwined. This point is developed further in the next study. '

## 5:7   Case J : TRAINING IN SOCIAL SKILLS

### BACKGROUND

Any person who is to supervise or manage people effectively must have considerable skill in handling and working with others. Training which aims to increase interpersonal effectiveness, allowing individuals to work better with other people, is usually given the slightly misleading name of "social skills training."

In recent years there has been an increasing use of social skills training involving such techniques as sensitivity training, role playing, task-oriented training groups and certain types of simulation exercise. The majority of these techniques utilise people working together in groups. Groups of this kind provide a powerful medium for training but also present the trainer with some awkward problems. Because of the large number of interactions between individual members of the training group, the trainer may have difficulty in identifying, let alone controlling, the progress of the group. Yet only by identifying and measuring those changes in behaviour which take place in social skills training can evaluation studies provide the feedback necessary to permit the trainer to establish control over the training situation.

### AIM

To devise a system for recording changes in the behaviour of individuals working in groups and to use this information to improve effectiveness of the training.

### THE STUDY

This study was carried out in an airline which was using task-oriented training groups as a method for developing the social skills of supervisory personnel. Training courses lasted for four or sometimes five days, and supervisors worked in groups of seven or eight. Each group was given a succession of tasks to complete, these varying from simple and unambiguous tasks to more complex tasks with a considerable ambiguity. In order to complete tasks successfully, the group had to work together, agreeing and actioning methods for task performance. During the course, which typically consisted of twenty-five or more tasks, members of a group became

practised in working together, and both they and their trainers
were regularly convinced that changes had taken place in the group's
behaviour although they were often unable to specify the nature or
extent.

## IDENTIFYING CHANGES IN BEHAVIOUR
The first problem was therefore to identify those types of behaviour
which were changed by the training. In order to do this, videotape
recordings were made of groups working at various stages of the
course. The videotapes were run through after the course to decide
whether any types of behaviour could be identified which showed
changes as the course progressed. From a detailed examination
of these recordings it was possible to produce a list of behaviours
which were changed as the course progressed and as groups began
to work together more effectively.

## BEHAVIOUR AS BASIS FOR FURTHER SESSIONS
This behaviour was then used as the basis of a record of what was
happening during further training sessions. The idea here was
to be able to identify salient group processes in order to provide
very prompt evaluation information for trainers. Trainers were
then in a position to modify later sessions on the basis of the
systematic feedback they had obtained. This procedure parallels
the rapid use of reaction evaluation in business games illustrated
in Case D, and takes further the idea of a self-correcting training
system which was examined in Case F; the method also involves
an extension of the observation techniques used in Case H in the
study of interviewing skills.

## FEEDING BACK BEHAVIOUR INFORMATION
However, in the airline investigation the evaluation data was used
in an additional way - one which is particularly appropriate for
social skills training. The information about each person's behaviour
in the descriptive categories was fed back from time to time to the
group members themselves. The trainees were then able to discuss
and interpret the changes taking place, and a relatively suspicion-
free atmosphere of criticism and comment was thereby created.

## CLASSIFICATION OF BEHAVIOUR
There is insufficient space here satisfactorily to describe in detail
the behaviour categories and the scoring system which were used.

But the basic idea is very simple: each piece of behaviour is placed into one of eleven categories - either by an observer during the training session or later from videotape recordings. Examples of the eleven categories are: helpful proposing, unhelpful proposing, supporting, building, clarifying, confusing and criticising. Since trainers can readily express their training objectives in terms of these categories - for example, more "clarifying" and less "confusing" is clearly desired - it is now possible to assess systematically the changes brought about by training.

In the airline study, for example, there were significant increases in the amount of clarifying and building behaviour, so that at the end of the course, groups were showing a higher percentage of these behaviours, while disagreeing, confusing, criticising and unhelpful proposing all fell off significantly as the course progressed. Later applications of the techniques (on subsequent courses) allowed the trainers to modify their approach by discarding inappropriate exercises, and to set the current course behaviours in the context of previously-obtained evaluation data.

COMMENTS

The information from the behaviour analysis approach to social skills training is useful in two ways. First, it can be fed back to groups in order to augment the regular training experience, and second, it can be used by the trainer as the basis of immediate outcome evaluation. Measures taken during the final sessions in a training series can be compared with those from early sessions in just the same way as post-test and pre-test scores from knowledge questionnaires were compared in Cases E, F and G. It is also possible to extend the observation system into managers' work situations to develop information about intermediate outcomes of social skills training. In these cases working groups (in committee or decision-making meetings) can be examined, and the observed patterns of behaviour can be related to training objectives and earlier measures.

5:8    CHANGES IN ATTITUDE

The five studies of immediate outcome evaluation already described deal with changes in knowledge or skill. But in addition to aiming at improvement in these two areas, trainers often hope to alter the attitudes or opinions that trainees hold. In this final section of Chapter 5 we describe one fairly simple procedure for measuring success in this field.

Perhaps the most widely known form of attitude measurement consists of a series of statements about a particular topic.  The people whose attitudes are being assessed are asked to what extent they agree or disagree with each of these statements.  The design of a valid scale of this type can be a very lengthy process, and (unlike a knowledge questionnaire of the kind discussed earlier) its construction can satisfactorily be undertaken only by suitably qualified personnel.  It would obviously be an asset to have some simpler method which a trainer could use to get a quick estimate of alteration in trainees' attitude.  The advantage would be all the greater if the method was sufficiently flexible for the trainer himself to be able to adjust it to suit his own purposes.

AIM
To investigate a method of attitude assessment which might meet the trainer's requirements of being simple to construct, quick to administer and easy to analyse.

THE STUDY
The method investigated is known in the psychological literature as the "semantic differential technique."  A more complete account of this technique is presented in the Appendix, but for now just its basic approach can be outlined.

DEFINITION OF ATTITUDE
An attitude is regarded as a compound of many separate opinions and feelings.  An attitude to work study, for example, might contain all of the following views:  it is extremely complicated, fairly reliable, reasonably accurate and rather overrated .  A training programme designed to change supervisors' attitudes to work study might aim to lead the trainees to feel that work study was not really so complicated, that it was very reliable, mostly accurate and not at all overrated.

MEASUREMENT OF OPINION
To gauge a person's overall attitude towards a topic it is necessary to measure some of the separate opinions which make up the total attitude;  and in order to assess if, or how, training has affected the overall attitude these separate opinions must be measured on a before-and-after basis.  Now suppose that each of these separate opinions is represented on a separate scale, rather like that shown in Figure 5:6.

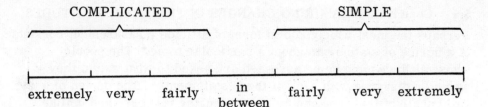

COMPLICATED                SIMPLE

extremely   very   fairly   in between   fairly   very   extremely

FIGURE 5:6 ATTITUDE TOWARDS A TOPIC

It would be easy for a person to indicate his opinion about how complicated he thinks work study is by placing a cross in one of the seven spaces on this scale. And a good impression of a person's overall attitude could be obtained by using further scales to assess those other opinions about work study – say its reliability, accuracy, usefulness, and so on, that are of interest to the trainer.

This approach has been used to examine the effects training programmes have had on supervisors' attitudes towards such subjects as work study, computers, safety and human relations. A different set of scales was of course required for each topic investigated since in each case different opinions were involved. These scales were developed through discussion with training staff and they were intended to cover the main opinion areas that the trainers were aiming to alter.

TRAINING OFFICERS AS TRAINEES

An example of one such study may help to clarify this point. On several occasions training programmes have taken place in which the trainees were themselves training officers. Where a contribution to the programme was on the subject of training evaluation, an attempt was made to measure the impact these efforts had on members' attitudes towards this subject. The form illustrated in Figure 5:7, made up of eight separate opinion scales, was used to assess the trainees' views on evaluation. Assessments were made on a before-and-after basis and a comparison of the two forms completed by each trainee showed whether or not their views had been affected by the session on evaluation.

The combined results for several training programmes are given in Figure 5:8. In all, 106 training officers took part in this study.

The words in the first two columns are those which appear at the end of the scales on the questionnaire form. One word of each pair is in capitals, and this indicates that the trainers aimed to move the trainees' opinions towards that end of the scale. A trainee's opinion on each scale could move in the direction desired

# THE EVALUATION OF TRAINING

Please give your opinion by putting a cross in the appropriate
space in each of the opinion scales below

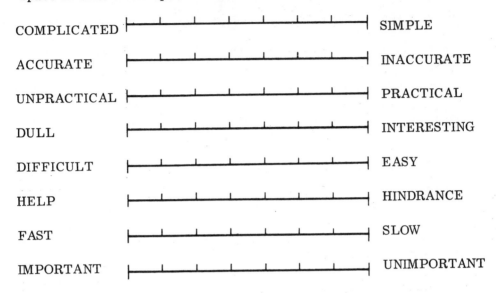

| | |
|---|---|
| COMPLICATED | SIMPLE |
| ACCURATE | INACCURATE |
| UNPRACTICAL | PRACTICAL |
| DULL | INTERESTING |
| DIFFICULT | EASY |
| HELP | HINDRANCE |
| FAST | SLOW |
| IMPORTANT | UNIMPORTANT |

FIGURE 5:7   FORM USED TO ASSESS OPINIONS ABOUT THE
EVALUATION OF TRAINING

by the trainer (a positive change), in the opposite direction ( a
negative change) or remain in the same position.  The number
of changes of each type (irrespective of their actual size) is given
in the three centre columns of the table.  The final two columns
represent the average view, on a pre- and post-test, of all the
trainees who took part in the study.  This was arrived at by numbering
each scale position from 1 to 7, so that the desirable opinion ( in
capitals) scored 7 in each case.  Taking the top row as an example,
it was hoped that the trainees would come to see evaluation as a
simpler process than before.

FINDINGS FROM FIGURE 5:8
Out of the 106 trainees, 51 of them shifted their opinion in the
desired direction while 19 moved the opposite way.  The opinions
of the remaining 36 were unchanged.  The average pre-test opinion
(2.8) corresponds to a view of evaluation as a fairly complicated
process.  The post-test position (3.5) indicates that there has been
a fairly sizeable overall shift of opinion towards the desirable end
of the scale.

E

| OPINION ADJECTIVES | | NUMBER OF: | | | AVERAGE POSITION | |
| --- | --- | --- | --- | --- | --- | --- |
| Left | Right | Positive changes | Negative changes | No change | Pre- test | Post test |
| complicated | SIMPLE | 51 | 19 | 36 | 2.8 | 3.5 |
| ACCURATE | inaccurate | 48 | 24 | 34 | 3.2 | 3.5 |
| unpractical | PRACTICAL | 47 | 20 | 39 | 4.9 | 5.3 |
| dull | INTERESTING | 30 | 27 | 49 | 5.6 | 5.7 |
| difficult | EASY | 52 | 21 | 33 | 2.5 | 3.4 |
| HELP | hindrance | 26 | 26 | 54 | 6.2 | 6.1 |
| FAST | slow | 44 | 21 | 41 | 3.9 | 4.2 |
| IMPORTANT | unimportant | 7 | 20 | 79 | 6.4 | 6.2 |
| | TOTALS | 305 | 178 | 365 | | |

FIGURE 5:8   CHANGES IN TRAINING OFFICERS' OPINIONS ABOUT EVALUATION

The pre-test position column shows that, as a group, the trainees initially viewed evaluation as interesting, helpful and important - scores of 5.6, 6.2 and 6.4 respectively, on the Seven-Point Scale. They believed it to be a fairly complicated, difficult and slow process, but despite this they saw it as a reasonably practical proposition. They also had doubts about the accuracy of the results of evaluation exercises. The information given them about evaluation led to some alteration in their views, and in the case of several opinions the majority of people changed in the required direction. Thus there was a tendency for the trainees subsequently to see evaluation as less complicated, difficult and slow. They also came to view evaluation as more practical and accurate. Overall there was virtually no change in opinions about its interest or helpfulness. Finally, there was a slight negative movement in beliefs about the importance of evaluation.

The last finding illustrates one of the major points to bear in mind when using the method. Most of the trainees, as the average pre-test position suggests, already regarded evaluation as highly important and had rated it in the most favourable position on the scale. It was impossible, therefore, for these trainees to indicate a positive change as their pre-test ratings were already on the extreme of the scale. This information is important to the trainer, since in such cases of high pre-test scores the training need not aim at changes in these particular opinions - emphasis may be placed on other opinion areas. This advantage of pre-test measurements has already been noted in the case of knowledge questionnaires, where pre-test scores were shown to provide information to the trainer about the level at which he should pitch his training.

COMMENTS

The method for measuring attitudes in terms of a set of opinions which was described in this study has the advantage of being simple to explain and easy both to administer and analyse. It is also a flexible technique, and the evaluator can readily adapt it to meet his own requirements.

Although it did not form part of the investigations, the permanence of attitude changes is likely to be of interest to the evaluator. The possibility of follow-up studies was mentioned under knowledge-gain evaluation, and there is no reason why attitudes also should not be retested some months after the end of the training period. This might be particularly informative, as the opinions a person holds are greatly influenced by the views of other people in his firm, particularly those of his immediate colleagues. A manager may find it difficult to retain attitudes that run counter to the prevailing "climate" of opinion in his works. This feature of the intermediate outcomes of training has been stressed in Chapter 2: change will be maintained only if it is relevant to the manager's job, and if his superiors and colleagues are receptive to the training he has received. These points are brought out in the next chapter.

# Chapter 6

# Intermediate Outcome Evaluation

It has been argued in previous chapters that the practising training officer might beneficially concentrate his evaluation efforts on the steps which precede intermediate outcomes. Changes in work behaviour are unquestionably the primary goal of management training, but this fact does not necessarily imply that trainers' evaluation work should be directed at measuring these changes. The themes that have been developed are these:

1       Intermediate outcome evaluation requires a considerable outlay of time and resources. If such an outlay is undertaken it will often have to be accompanied by a reduction of effort in other important areas

2       Managers' behaviour at work is determined by several crucial factors whose operation might lead to a quite false picture of how good training had been. This point is expanded below

3       Evaluation efforts directed to context, input, reaction and immediate outcome evaluation can almost guarantee that intermediate outcomes will be good ones. This argument has been presented in Chapter 2, and will be resumed in the final chapter

In this chapter three studies of intermediate outcome evaluation are described. It is hoped that they will illustrate techniques helpful to evaluators who feel they have time to examine changes in work behaviour. At the same time the studies will exemplify the points made above.

6:1    Case L : AN INVESTIGATION OF REPORTED CHANGES IN
              SUPERVISORS' WORK BEHAVIOUR

BACKGROUND
A large steel group ran residential courses lasting a fortnight for its supervisory staff. These included not only foremen from production and maintenance sections but also persons of similar standing from laboratories, drawing offices, clerical departments, and so on. Each course was centred around a particular production process - such as steelmaking, machining or rolling - and since the

jobs of all members of a course were associated with that particular process all trainees had a certain amount of common experience. The courses were held at the headquarters of the organisation, and this training was in addition to any the trainees might have received at their own branches of the firm. Although the training had other objectives - such as bringing supervisors up to date about certain aspects of the organisation's policy and future plans - the training staff hoped that they were also providing trainees with the kind of information and ideas that were likely to be of immediate practical use to them in their current jobs. The purpose of this study was to help the trainers to find out whether or not the training was achieving this result.

AIMS
1    To discover to what extent supervisors made changes in their work behaviour after attending a training programme
2    To investigate certain other factors that might influence the outcome of the training

THE STUDY
This study involved the members of three separate training courses (a fuller account of this investigation is presented in M W Bird, "Changes in Work Behaviour Following Supervisory Training," Journal of Management Studies, 1969, 6, 331-45). At the beginning of their course, trainees were invited to participate in an evaluation exercise which was then explained to them. They were told that the training staff hoped that while undergoing training they would absorb inform- ation that would help them carry out their own jobs more effectively. At the end of the course, each trainee would be asked to write a brief description of one change he proposed to make in his work method as a result of an idea he had acquired during the training. The evaluator would keep a record of each change described and the trainee, too, would retain a copy. A few months later the evaluator would visit each trainee to inquire whether or not he had been successful in introducing the change.

THE FOLLOW-UP
Thirty-three trainees provided the evaluator with a proposed change at the end of their training. A further eleven claimed that the training had provided them with no fresh ideas about their jobs.

When the evaluator later interviewed each supervisor who had outlined a proposed change, he asked him not only about how he had fared with this change but also if he had tried to introduce any other change which had originated from ideas arising out of the training. As well as collecting information about changes that had been successful introduced, details were also requested about changes that, for some reason, the supervisor had found he was unable to accomplish. The evaluator also asked trainees about certain other factors, in particular about the amount of interest his immediate superior had shown in the training. This latter was judged on the extent of the manager's briefing and de-briefing of his supervisor immediately before and after he attended the training course. We may take this as a simple measure of the "leadership climate" in which the supervisor is operating. Finally the manager of each trainee was asked about the degree to which the supervisor demonstrated an initiative to introduce change – that is to say, how frequently he tried out or suggested possible ways of improving on the effectiveness of his section.

The average number of work changes made was approximately two per supervisor, but whereas some had successfully introduced up to six changes others had achieved only one. Examples of changes made were:

1    Regular safety inspections of section started
2    Simple work-study techniques employed
3    Training programme for subordinates drawn up
4    Control procedure for consumable stores improved

There was thus no doubt that the training had produced some changes in work behaviour. As far as intermediate outcome evaluation was concerned, however, it was naturally difficult to put any absolute value on the numbers of changes observed. Whether an average of two changes is a good or bad score is still undecided. The answer can only be relative to outcomes of other similar courses.


THE CHIEF FEATURE OF THE STUDY
The main importance of this study derives from its interest in factors affecting the intermediate success of training. When the change scores of individual trainees were examined in relation to other factors, the following picture emerged:
1    Foremen tended to introduce more changes than did the other types of supervisors on the training programme. A majority of the latter group held the view that the training in question was slanted towards the needs of trainees who were directly involved in the production process
2    Supervisors who in their managers' opinions possessed high "change initiative" achieved more as a result of their training

than did those whose personality (as judged by their boss) was less outgoing

3    The "leadership climate" in which the intermediate outcomes were measured proved also to be crucial. As was noted above, this climate was measured in terms of how interested a trainee's boss was in the training provided. The influence of this factor was clear-cut: the greater the boss's interest, the more changes introduced after training

4    Another important organisational factor operated in the following way: supervisors engaged on shift work were found to have met more difficulty than non-shift supervisors in utilising their training. This was because the jobs of shift foremen were often closely linked with those of the foremen on the other shifts, so that agreement over three shifts was required before changes could be introduced

## COMMENTS

This study indicates plainly that the intermediate outcomes of training depend on factors other than those arising from the training process itself. The leadership and organisational climate (here in terms of boss's interest and the shift system) clearly matter, as does a trainee's personality - here in terms of change initiative. Training given to a rather conservative supervisor who lacks support and positive encouragement from his boss and colleagues has a very limited chance of intermediate success - even though it may be a very good training programme. This illustrates the argument about the value of intermediate outcome evaluation: in many cases a measure of intermediate outcomes is not a fair measure of the effectiveness of training itself. Perhaps importance should be given to creating the right context for training and then the more practicable process of immediate outcome evaluation should be emphasised.

One procedural feature of the present study may be applicable elsewhere. Trainees' awareness that they were subsequently to be interviewed about changes they had tried to implement was probably important in increasing the effectiveness of the training. This effect was all the greater because trainees had written down details at the end of the training of hoped-for changes in their work situation. Follow-up interviews are clearly of value in this situation, if time is available to carry them out. But, as in so many other cases, their value is as a means of improving training rather than simply as a means of obtaining evaluation material.

BACKGROUND

At an early stage in the training process the trainer must set his
objectives. He then has to decide which are the most appropriate
training techniques to use in order to achieve these objectives.
Unfortunately the lack of information about the relative merits of
different training procedures means that there is little to guide the
trainer in his choice.

AIM

To compare two different methods of safety training for supervisors.
The number of job changes resulting from each method was to be
used as the criterion of effectiveness.

THE STUDY

A chemical company, dissatisfied with its existing TWI based three-
day residential safety training course, decided to try a completely new
approach. The training staff were anxious to evaluate both methods
carefully so that in future they could opt for the better one. After
discussion it was agreed that a suitable criterion of success would
be the number of changes which a supervisor made in his job as a
result of the training. Because not all changes are equally important,
it was decided that each change would be rated by the firm's safety
officer using a five-point scale. The categories were as follows:

1    A very small change unlikely to affect the safety of the
     section in any way - for example, removing an old notice from
     the board
2    A small change but one which could affect the safety of the
     section - for example, removing a piece of broken glass from
     the gangway
3    A larger change requiring more effort but not necessarily
     having much effect on safety - for example, marking out
     gangways in the section more clearly
4    A larger change requiring more effort which would be likely
     to improve the safety of the section - for example, a complete
     check on all safety equipment, lifting gear and so on
5    A fundamental change almost certain to improve the safety
     of the section - for example, redesigning or repositioning
     dangerous plant, introduction of new safety procedures, etc

## THE SAFETY PROJECT APPROACH

The new training approach consisted of a safety project. Supervisors undergoing training were split up into groups of four. Each group was told to carry out a two-day safety survey of a particular area of the works and to report on the hazards they discovered. Supervisors were not sent to investigate an area in which they worked. The old procedure was a three-day residential safety course without any on-the-job hazard spotting exercise. Twenty-one supervisors on the residential course were followed up on the job and asked to list every change made by them since the training, which might have improved the safety of their section, however large or small that change might be. They were given examples of possible exchanges both minor and major. This follow-up took place one month after the course. An identical procedure was used to record the changes made by supervisors who had taken part in the new project system of training. The results were as in Figure 6:1.

| | NUMBER OF TRAINEES | NUMBER OF CHANGES | AVERAGE | IMPORTANCE OF CHANGES | | | | |
|---|---|---|---|---|---|---|---|---|
| | | | | 1 | 2 | 3 | 4 | 5 |
| OLD METHOD | 21 | 34 | 1.6 | 3 | 19 | 12 | - | - |
| PROJECT METHOD | 16 | 143 | 8.9 | 38 | 64 | 25 | 14 | 2 |

FIGURE 6:1  A COMPARISON OF TWO SAFETY TRAINING METHODS

These findings show, that judged on the number of job changes made, the project method was distinctly superior. It gave an average of 8.9 changes per supervisor compared with the average of 1.6 changes coming from the old training method. In terms of quality, there is very little difference in the average group having an average value of 2.1 on the five-point scale described earlier, and the old method group having an average of 2.2. However, it can be seen that in categories 4 and 5, which represent major job changes, only the project method group achieved any score.

## COMMENTS

On the evidence of this study the project method emerges as much the more successful training technique. However, this judgement is based strictly on its effectiveness in producing changes in supervisors' work behaviour and may not apply in different circumstances. In might well be that the other method would have proved the better if the basis of comparison had been improvement in knowledge of the Factories Act or of the company's safety policy. This is another illustration of the point that there are many forms of evaluation. Training staff need to decide before a programme is arranged which form of evaluation is the one they are most interested in.

TWO ASPECTS OF EVALUATION

In fact the present study itself involved two aspects of evaluation. The investigation of job changes was an example of intermediate outcome evaluation. In addition, the effectiveness of two distinct training methods was being compared. Insofar as interest was focused on the relative merits of the two techniques for attaining particular objectives then this study qualifies also as input evaluation. Training methods (inputs) must generally be assessed in terms of the results they achieve. So any input evaluation will almost certainly involve an element of outcome evaluation too. In some instances, as in this study, the two evaluation processes will be going on side by side. In other cases of input evaluation the trainer will be drawing upon his experience of previous outcome evaluations when deciding which training method seems most likely to suit his purpose. But either way, input evaluation is impossible without some reference to trainees' reactions or training outcomes.

6:3   Case N : A STUDY OF CHANGES IN WORK PERFORMANCE
            USING EVIDENCE FROM TWO SOURCES

BACKGROUND

The two studies of intermediate outcomes just described relied upon evidence of change provided by the trainees themselves. The trainees' managers, who are generally in a good position to notice if any work changes take place following training, were not asked for information about the effects of training. The study now to be described included independent reports from both trainees and their managers so that it was possible to see if their separate accounts tallied.

The training evaluated was a four-week programme put on by a large organisation for certain of its junior managers. The average age of the eighteen trainees was just under thirty, they were of HNC or degree standard in education and all were expected to be strong candidates for promotion in the future. This was the first occasion that an attempt had been made to provide appropriate training for this grade and calibre of manager within the organisation.  Previously such managers would have had to attend some external course if they were to receive training of the standard planned.  As this was a new venture for the training staff they were interested in discovering how far their efforts had been successful.

AIMS
1    To discover if the trainees' superiors reported improvements to work performance following the training
2    To obtain the trainees' views on the benefits they felt had come from the training
3    To discover the degree of agreement between the reports coming from these two sources

THE STUDY
An appraisal form was drawn up containing sixty-one items, each of which defined a particular area of managerial work.  The items were based on a study of the course programme and discussions with the training staff.  Each of the sixty-one items could be classified under one of the following six categories.  An example item is included for each category:

1    Background.  Understanding of the policies and organisation of the company
2    Financial.  Ability to operate cost and budget control procedures
3    Organisational.  Ability to arrange and cope with changes in work procedures
4    Personnel.  Ability to co-operate effectively with members of other departments. (This category was in practice divided into sub-classes covering subordinates, superiors, and personnel of other departments.)
5    Technical.  Understanding of the plant, processes, and so on, under his control
6    Personal skills.  Ability to put forward constructive ideas and suggestions

On two occasions each trainee's manager was asked to appraise the performance of his subordinate on each of the sixty-one items.  He did this first while the course was in progress to indicate the trainee's pre-training standard and then again some six months later.  Assessments were made on a six-point scale ranging from "average" to "very good." There were no positions on the scale for below-average performance, as experience has shown that below-average positions on appraisal forms are rarely used by assessors in studies of this grade of trainee.

A comparison between the two appraisals of a particular trainee would show if there had been any change in his performance since the training. However, given the calibre of the trainees their performance might well have improved over six months, even if they had not received any formal training. It was then necessary to obtain similar information about a small group of people comparable in age, ability and grade to the trainees. So a control group of people not receiving any training was set up by asking four managers to appraise a member of their staff who was similar in character to the trainees. Two appraisals were made by each control group manager, again covering a six-month period, on forms identical to those used by the trainees' managers.

THE FINDINGS

From an examination of the managers' appraisals it was clear that the trainees had improved considerably more than the people in the control group. In thirty-seven of the sixty-one items there was evidence of significant improvements in the trainees' performance. Most improvements were in the personnel, organisational and personal skills categories. Two of the other categories are of particular interest. The financial items revealed only a few changes, and it is likely that this was because trainees were in fact not concerned with financial aspects of their departments. The technical items revealed no improvements at all. This was gratifying, since these items were included as a test of the evaluation method rather than of the training. The training had had a negligible technical content, and a check was needed on whether the managers completing the forms were showing a response bias towards favourable judgements of all kinds. This was not so, and confidence in the other results therefore further increased.

JUDGEMENTS OF THE TRAINER

Each trainee was asked twice for his views on the value (to him personally) of the training. They gave their answers on forms containing the same sixty-one items as were listed on the appraisal forms. Immediately after the course trainees were asked to what extent they felt the training had increased their knowledge of the work described in each item. A six-point scale extending from "no-change" to "greatly improved" was provided for their answers. Six months later trainees were sent a similar form and asked on which items they felt their work had improved as a result of what they had learned during the training. Again a six-point scale was used for their answers.

The questions posed to the trainees were thus rather different on the two occasions that they gave their views on the outcome of the training. However, if their replies were valid a certain consistency between the two sets of answers was to be expected. For without some initial learning during the course there would be no grounds later for claiming that performance had improved as a result of information acquired during training. There was in fact a pleasing consistency in their answers: items where considerable learning was reported during the course tended to be the items on which work performance was later said to have improved and vice versa.

A final question is as follows: did managers' and trainees' estimate of improvements differ? Whereas the managers' appraisals indicated that there had been significant improvement in performance on thirty-seven items, the trainees' accounts were rather more conservative, pointing to improvements on only thirty items. Nor were the same items necessarily present in the list of improvements from both sources. But again the agreement outweighed the discrepancies. Of the thirty items on the trainees' list of changes, twenty-four were contained within the thirty-seven items on which managers judged improvements to have occurred. So on the basis of the evidence available from both sources, it is highly likely that for these twenty-four items at least, the training had enhanced the trainees' performance. (Another aspect of this study - not reported here - involved obtaining managers' rating of the importance of each of the sixty-one items. It may be briefly noted that the majority of changes had occurred in job areas thought by individual bosses to be important ones.)

COMMENTS

As happened with the previous case, this study embraced two forms of evaluation. The judgements of trainees at the end of the course may be viewed as reaction level evaluation, whilst the information from the managers' and trainees' later comments may be treated as intermediate outcome evaluation. This study has shown how reaction level information (the expressed views of trainees about their training) can accurately predict where intermediate level changes will in fact occur.

The second important feature of these results is the observed consistency between information provided by trainees and that from their managers. In many situations it is impracticable to obtain both sets of information, and an evaluator might wonder how the material he has collected agrees with the other possible set. This investigation suggests that an acceptable degree of overlap may be assumed.

Factors influencing intermediate outcomes were not in this study examined as they were in Case L. It must be presumed that differences in leadership climate and in trainees' personality were again contributory factors, but one general difference between the studies is noteworthy. The level and calibre of managers in this study was higher than that of the trainees in Case L. It appeared that the present managers were meeting fewer obstacles in their application of training material, probably because of their greater scope for personal initiative and their more considerable powers of persuasion.

# Part III

# LESSONS OF THE STUDIES

# Chapter 7

# Practical Conclusions

It will be clear that there is no one answer to the question "Was this management training programme a success?" The several possible types of answer within the C I R O framework described in Chapter 1 have already been enumerated. This framework embodies the following types of evaluation:

1    Context evaluation
2    Input evaluation
3    Reaction evaluation
4    Outcome evaluation
  (a)  Immediate outcomes
  (b)  Intermediate outcomes
  (c)  Ultimate outcomes

## 7 1    PICKING THE RIGHT EVALUATION QUESTIONS

A training officer, therefore, has to select which specific evaluation questions he wishes to ask. It has been suggested that questions about ultimate outcome evaluation are usually unanswerable, since so many different factors contribute to departmental or company success: the training of a particular manager is only one small item among a collection of contributing factors. There is, however, one circumstance where ultimate outcome evaluation is worth while. When a broad range of members of a department are being trained as part of a single programme, the ultimate effectiveness of that collective programme may well be measured in terms of departmental productivity figures.

## VALUE OF INTERMEDIATE OUTCOME EVALUATION
Should a training officer try to answer questions about intermediate outcomes? It has been argued that there are major differences between operative and management training; and that, whereas operative training may be evaluated in terms of intermediate consequences, such an approach to management training is often much less sensible. A manager's behaviour at work is determined by a variety of factors, so that training is only one contributory factor among many. To examine the effectiveness of a single training course by looking at

F

trainees' behaviour at work can lead to conclusions which are unfair to the course organisers. On the other hand, intermediate outcome evaluation studies are particularly appropriate when it is a whole system of training (rather than a specific single course) which is being assessed. In these situations (where several members of a department are all being trained together, for instance), behaviour at work is a much more reliable index of training effectiveness.

FACTORS INFLUENCING BEHAVIOUR

This can be related to the discussion in Chapter 2 of the factors influencing a manager's work behaviour   Among these factors are the following:

1    The success of training at an immediate outcome level
2    The relevance of training on the job
3    The leadership and organisational climate
4    The manager's own personality and motivation
5    His subordinates

When an interlocking system of training for groups of managers and subordinates is in operation, factors 2, 3 and 5 of those above are clearly being dealt with. On the other hand, individual training programmes for individual managers are inclined to leave them aside. As has been seen in Chapter 6, this can be a mistake.

There is no doubt that in many cases an emphasis on immediate outcome evaluation combined with context, input and reaction evaluation work is the one best geared to ensure that the intermediate outcomes of management training are good ones. Context evaluation includes examination of the crucial factors 2, 3 and 5 listed in the previous paragraph. Once these have been tackled, and factor 1 (immediate outcomes) is satisfactory, the intermediate outcomes can almost be left to look after themselves.

Context evaluation is thus undeniably central to any training process. In the same way input evaluation is also vital. Indeed a training programme cannot possibly be organised without someone gathering information about training resources in order to choose between alternative "inputs." Turning to reaction evaluation, it might be considered that this is sufficiently straightforward and productive for it to be employed fairly regularly. But (as with any other type of evaluation) relying entirely on reaction measures would be unwise.

7:2    COLLECTION OF OUTCOME EVALUATION DATA

As well as the three forms of evaluation noted in the previous paragraph, it will usually be essential for evaluators to obtain some measure of the outcomes of training. But it does not follow from this that the procedures discussed in Chapter 5 and 6 need to be applied in the case of every management training programme. An inflexible rule, "outcome evaluation must always take place," is not desirable as the decision depends very largely upon the situation. Several features of a training situation which may influence decisions about how much outcome evaluation to attempt should be noted.

IMPORTANCE OF TRAINING PROGRAMMES
The first factor is the relative importance of the training programmes which a department is running. Some programmes will be put on at regular intervals for key personnel - a graduate entrants' induction course, for instance. The potential benefits from evaluating the outcome of this type of programme are obviously considerably greater than those from investigating a one-off course which is unlikely to be repeated. But even the important courses need not be evaluated every time. Once a course is established, checks can be made at intervals to ensure that training standards are being maintained. It is during the development phase of a new programme that evaluation is most necessary; if during its first few occasions the programme can be treated as a self-correcting training system (see Case F in Chapter 5), evaluation will be serving its true purpose.

NATURE OF INFORMATION COLLECTED
The second factor determining the value of outcome evaluation is the nature of the information which can be collected. It is obvious that the information must be reliable, but, more important, it must be useful. Information need not be collected unless it can be used to improve training.

AVAILABLE RESOURCES
Third, the training department's resources naturally affect its decisions about evaluation. Many departments work under considerable pressure, and cannot be expected to measure the outcomes of all their efforts. In some instances (above) outcome evaluation material is worth collecting, but in almost all cases context, input and reaction evaluation should be carried out.

THE VALUE OF OUTSIDE HELP
A fourth point concerns the outside help or co-operation which training staff can anticipate. Evaluation can rarely be carried out without the assistance of people outside the training department. In some cases,

particularly in reaction and immediate outcome evaluation, these will be the trainees themselves. Intermediate outcome evaluation will require co-operation from trainees' managers and from other departments - the safety officer might be asked to provide accident figures, for example. It is clear that trainers' relations with these other departments must affect the kind of outcome evaluation they can attempt. But in all cases the early enlistment of outside help in the planning of evaluation work should be encouraged.

## 7:3   REACTION AND INPUT EVALUATION

Input evaluation deserves a rather more extensive treatment than it has received so far. In Figure 1:1 it was defined in terms of "obtaining and using information about possible training resources in order to choose between alternative inputs to training." Training inputs are of course very varied; in the case of in-company courses one may be concerned with access to visual aids, to case study material or even to visiting speakers.

### REACTIONS TO EXTERNAL COURSES

These particular issues are less salient in the case of training presented by organisations external to the company. In these instances it has been assumed that the organisers can provide the materials and the means of delivery, and input evaluation becomes more a question of assessing the opinions of people who have had experience of the programme which is offered. It is here that the link between reaction and input evaluation becomes obvious; input evaluation on these occasions largely comprises decision-making on the basis of reaction evaluation data.

When training staff are faced with a choice between external courses, the input evaluation work would be greatly simplified if they had access to systematically collected material about the views and recommendations of personnel who had previously attended these courses. At the present time there are in operation two input evaluation services of this kind.

### THE DE LA RUE INDEX

The De La Rue Index (P O  Box 2, De La Rue House, 84 Regent Street, London W 1) works through member companies in this way Each company that joins the scheme is issued with a supply of standard reaction evaluation forms. These are completed by delegates attending external training courses and a copy of each completed form is returned to the De La Rue Index.

The reaction forms contain sections where a course member can describe the organisation and structure of the course, its stated objectives and the administrative arrangements. He is asked to express an opinion about the speakers, the teaching procedures and the course content, as well as to comment on how far he felt that the course achieved its aim.

The Index organisers collate the information obtained about available courses, and member companies have access to this information as they request it. It is also possible to obtain the opinions which have been gathered about particular lecturers over and above the measured reactions to courses as a whole.

## BIM COURSE ASSESSMENT SCHEME

The British Institute of Management (Management Education Information Unit, BIM, Management House, Parker Street, London WC 2) has recently commenced a similar scheme for management training courses which is open to member companies. Their assessment questionnaire contains items about the aims, content, length and administration of a course, and the teaching aids which were employed, as well as allowing for opinions about individual speakers.

## THE VALUE OF THESE SCHEMES

It is apparent that schemes of this kind can play an important role in systematic input evaluation. Their success does of course depend upon a constant flow of up-to-date information to and from companies, and this is only as meaningful as the standard questionnaires allow. In this respect it is encouraging to note that both organisations appear to adopt a flexible approach to information collection.

It must, however, be stressed that the information which is provided does not extend to outcome evaluation material. Data on the outcomes of training are extremely difficult for a central organisation to obtain and it is to be hoped that external course organisers themselves will turn more to the collection of immediate outcome information – and that, having collected it, they will apply it along the lines of the self-correcting system approach.

## 7:4   EVALUATION IS PART OF TRAINING

One theme of this book is that evaluation is not something which happens after training has finished. Evaluation is an integral part of training, so that a trainer who is doing his job well is necessarily evaluating his success at the same time.

This fundamental point may perhaps be illustrated by the thirteen case studies presented in Chapters 3, 4, 5 and 6. These were designed primarily as an evaluation exercise, but each of them has clear implications about training procedures. The first two cases were of context evaluation, and the methods employed for identifying training needs are central to any such work. Reaction evaluation material (Cases C, D, and N) is regularly used to improve training possibly along the lines of a self-correcting training system (Case F) Such a system may well be based upon attitude-change information (Case K) or upon follow-up information gathered from trainees' work situations (Case M). Obtaining information and feeding it back into training can help that training (Case J) and evaluation work will often suggest better ways to train (Case H). The very act of trainees' supplying information may lead them to learn more (Case G) or to introduce more changes in their work-place (Case L). And evaluation work may reveal significant differences between, say, older and younger trainees in their ability to profit from a particular form of training (Case E).

In all these ways, then, evaluation is not carried out for its own sake - it is carried out for the sake of training.

## 7:5   CONCLUDING REMARKS

The needs of the trainer for systematically-gathered information has been repeatedly stressed, particularly for the sort of information that will help him both to control the training process and to make it more effective. This book has presented a framework for describing the variety of evaluation information which may be collected, and it has illustrated the ways in which the framework may be applied in practical situations.

It would be unrealistic to expect that all the methods outlined could be transplanted indiscriminately into all management training situations without some risk of rejection. The intention has been to set down some experiences in management training evaluation in the hope that these might provide others with some clues about how to tackle the problems posed by their own training situation. There is nothing sacrosanct about the techniques described in this book. They are all open to adaptation and modification, and trainers should not hesitate to do this if they believe it will be to their advantage. And should any trainers so despair of the limitations of the techniques described here that they feel obliged to design their own from scratch, this is all to the good. For evaluation methods for use in management training are relatively scarce at present and any practicable additions to the list will be welcomed.

Earlier in the book reference was made to this extract from a

Central Training Council report ("Training and Development of Managers: Further Proposals," a report by the Management Training and Development Committee of the Central Training Council, London, HMSO, 1969): "The effectiveness of management training at managerial levels is difficult to assess and often impossible to measure." It seems appropriate to conclude by quoting the sentence which follows it. "But unless the attempt is made, useful lessons may go unlearnt, the planning of future programmes may suffer, and valuable resources in terms of managerial time and effort may be wasted."

# APPENDIX

# Construction and Use of Questionnaires

Throughout this book there has been an emphasis on the need for control information. The evaluation studies which have been described all hinged on our being able to measure what was happening at certain stages of the training process. The measures used were occasionally of a somewhat makeshift kind, but they always were adequate to play their part in decisions about training. A common feature was the reliance on some form of questionnaire to learn about opinions, attitudes, knowledge, or descriptions of people's behaviour. Such questionnaires have usually to be developed and used by an evaluator himself; and it is the purpose of this Appendix to provide some practical guidance in these operations.

The three principal types of questionnaire which have been described are:

1    Opinion and attitude measures
2    Session assessment forms
3    Knowledge questionnaires

The construction and use of each of these will be discussed in turn. Finally the question of whether or not trainees should put their name on forms they complete as part of an evaluation exercise will be examined.

## A1  ATTITUDE MEASURES

An alteration of trainees' attitudes is a frequent training objective, and the trainer who wishes to assess what immediate changes have taken place might consider using the simple and acceptable method which was outlined in Case K. With very little modification this method can also be used to monitor attitudes over long periods in the work situation.

### DEFINITION OF ATTITUDE
The technique (known as the "semantic differential" procedure) depends on the definition of an "attitude" in terms of a set of "opinions." Each

"opinion" may be measured by a rating scale, and the overall pattern of a person's scale responses makes up his "attitude." This procedure is quite widely used by psychologists in many fields. So far as training evaluation is concerned, the opinion scales have to be selected to cover the main aims of the training programme, so that different scales will obviously be used according to the topic which is under consideration.

At this point it will be helpful to look back to Figure 5:7. This contains a set of rating scales which have been used to measure trainees opinions about the evaluation of training. But it should be emphasised at the outset that people's attitudes to most issues can be measured in this way - by naming the issue at the top of the page and by selecting an appropriate set of opinion scales.

## A2   CONSTRUCTING THE QUESTIONNAIRE

When a training officer has decided which attitude-area he wishes to examine, he first has to pick an appropriate descriptive term to place at the head of the form. This term may be a general one - for example "computers" or "shop stewards" - or it may be rather more specific to current activies in the organisation - for instance, "the company's new wages structure" or "the introduction of management by objectives." The term to be picked will obviously depend upon the training programme which is being developed. An example about a work study appreciation course will serve as an adequate basis for discussion at this point.

### LOOKED-FOR RESULTS OF WORK STUDY COURSE

The training officer who wishes to assess changes in opinions about work study following a course on this subject must next decide in what respects he is wanting to change opinions. It is fairly clear, for example, that he will want trainees to feel that work study is "less complicated" as a result of their training. So he might start with the opinion scale "complicated - simple." Notice that this involves using a pair of words, one of which is roughly the opposite of the other. The training officer's task at this point is therefore to decide on as many pairs of words as he thinks are important for his training goals. At the same time he should decide which of the two words of each pair comes nearer to his aim - which one, in other words, represents the answer he ideally wants after training.

The pairs of words should then be laid out as in Figure 5:7. Seven spaces along the scale between each pair of words are recommended. The sequence of the scales is unimportant (alphabetical order is one

possibility), but the direction of each pair is of some consequence.
It is ill-advised to have all the desirable words down one side of the
page, and the best procedure is to mix up the direction of the pairs
in a random fashion. In Figure 5:7 for instance, the desirable words
are "simple" (to the right of the page), "accurate" (to the left),
"practical" (to the right), "interesting" (to the right), and so on.

## A3   USING AND SCORING THE QUESTIONNAIRE

As the trainer will be interested in the way attitudes have changed,
he will have to ask trainees to complete the questionnaire on at least
two occasions for him to be able to see any shift in the pattern of
answers. This will usually involve a pre-test shortly before training
begins followed by a post-test immediately after it is completed. The
trainer must remember, when assessing the results of such a study,
that large changes immediately after training may not always be maintained for long periods afterwards, but that a training programme which
fails to generate any immediate changes over its duration is one which
needs amending.

### FILLING UP THE FORM

How does a person fill up this form? Consider the rating of work
study on the scale "complicated - simple." Each of the seven divisions
on the line separating these adjectives represents a transition between
viewing work study as "complicated" and viewing it as "simple." A
trainee gives his opinion by making a mark (a tick or a cross) in one
of these seven spaces according to how complicated or simple he considers
work study to be. The fourth space along (from either end) is the mid-
point, and spaces which are progressively further out indicate
progressively more simple and more complicated judgements. In this
way the seven divisions along the line have the approximate meaning
shown in Figure A1.

   If a person put his mark in space 5 this would indicate that to him
work study seemed "fairly simple."

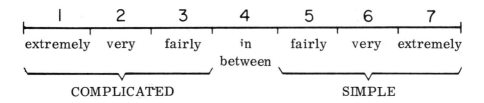

FIGURE A1 : SPECIMEN SCALE : "COMPLICATED - SIMPLE"

The trainer will need to take some time over explaining the nature of the questionnaire to the trainees and in telling them carefully what he wants them to do. But after this, people should be encouraged to fill in the rating scales fairly rapidly. In describing how to use the form a training officer should ask for first, quick opinions. As a rough guide, an eight-scale form ( as in Figure 5:7) should be completed in under a minute.

SCORING THE ANSWERS

What about scoring the answers obtained before and after a training programme? It will be noticed that the "complicated - simple" scale in Figure A1 has been numbered from 1 to 7. It is on this basis that a numerical value is given to the space which a person marks. The desirable word of a pair (simple, accurate, practical, interesting and so on in Figure 5:7), is given a value of 7, and the other word is scored 1. With 4 as the mid-point, 2 and 3 and 5 and 6 are intermediate placements. This means that when trainees have completed the scales, their answers have to be changed into numbers. The best procedure here is to write all the scores down on a large sheet of paper. In this way the result might be as shown in Figure A2 .

PERSONS COMPLETING THE FORM

| RATING SCALES | A Brown | | | B Smith | | |
|---|---|---|---|---|---|---|
| | Pre | Post | Change | Pre | Post | Change |
| "complicated - simple" | 2 | | | 4 | | |
| | | 4 | | | 3 | |
| | | | 2 | | | -1 |
| "inaccurate - accurate" | 5 | | | 5 | | |
| | | 5 | | | 6 | |
| | | | 0 | | | 1 |
| "unpractical - practical" | 3 | | | 3 | | |
| | | 2 | | | 4 | |
| | | | -1 | | | 1 |

FIGURE A2   SPECIMEN LAYOUT OF QUESTIONNAIRE ANSWERS
SHOWN NUMERICALLY

Staggering the entry of pre-test, post-test and change scores enables the trainer to add across rows easily. Thus if he wishes to obtain the average pre-test mark on the "complicated - simple" scale he totals the figures in the top row and then divides by the number of trainees. Under this system of scoring a positive change of opinion results in the post-test score being higher than the pre-test.

GETTING THE BEST OUT OF THE TABULAR MATTER
Once scores have been tabulated in this way they can be used to assess a training programme's effectiveness in changing opinions. A suitable procedure is to look at each rating scale separately. First, the average pre-test and the average post-test score for all trainees on the scale can be calculated and the average change observed; then the number of trainees moving in the desired direction on each scale can be noted, with the number not changing and the number who move in the opposite direction. An example of a set of results from such an analysis is given in Figure 5:8. At that point, too, attention is drawn to the need to examine pre-test positions, since a very high pre-test score may itself preclude any change due to training.

Using these attitude rating scales is extremely simple. Not only does the method provide a rapid overall impression of the effectiveness of a programme by showing the number of scales with frequent changes in the desired direction, but it also points to any differences between the several rating scales. As an illustration of this second possibility, consider the case where a work study appreciation course results in clear, positive opinion-change on the scales "accurate - inaccurate" and "complicated - simple" but no consistent movement on scales like "important - unimportant," "help - hindrance," and "necessary - unnecessary." If this is coupled with low scores in these scales, the results would imply that trainess have come to recognise the accuracy and relative simplicity of work study, but that they have not been persuaded of its worth in their department. In these conditions the appreciation course has in part failed, and appropriate changes would need to be tried in later training programmes.

A4 SESSION ASSESSMENT FORMS

The attitude rating scales discussed above are primarily for assessing some of the immediate outcomes of a training programme. A very similar procedure can, however, be used to discover trainees' reactions to a training programme. (See Case Studies C and D.) This particular procedure involves what have earlier been called "session assessment forms."

An example of one of these forms appears in Figure 4:1. The princip behind these scales is similar to that discussed in the previous section. Each trainee independently completes one of these forms at the end of each session of a training programme, or, if the programme is not divided into discrete units, at appropriate intervals during the training.

## CONSTRUCTING THE FORMS

Constructing a session assessment form presents no problems. The three basic scales illustrated in Figure 4:1 may be sufficient, but trainers are, of course, at liberty to choose other scales which interest them. Special session assessment forms have also been used, for instance, for group discussion work. Here scales were incorporated asking how effective each trainee thought his own contributions to be, how satisfied he was with the group atmosphere, how far he felt involved in the success or failure of the group, as well as other related questions. Note also that an "any further comments" space on a session assessment form can be illuminating; trainees should be encouraged to write down any other opinions in more detail than is possible on the scale.

## SEPARATE SESSION ASSESSMENT FORMS NEEDED

Much of what was said above about attitude rating questionnaires applies also to session assessment forms, and the details need not be repeated. In the case of session assessment forms, however, there is an obvious necessity for as many separate forms per trainee as there are distinct sessions. For a week's programme upwards of twenty forms might be needed for each trainee. It is helpful, therefore, to provide booklets of forms stapled together at the outset, each form being headed with the title of a session. Trainees can retain their booklet throughout the course, though they should be encouraged to complete a form immediately at the end of each session. This quite rapidly becomes part of a course procedure.

Scoring session assessment forms follow similar lines to those set down above for attitude ratings. Obviously in these situations the trainer will not be concerned about pre- and post-tests so the scoring system will be that much simpler. In addition the comments provided by course members can often be very useful and might show, for example, that a speaker was inaudible or that his slides were not at all clear from the back of the room.

## THE SYSTEM OF RANK-ORDERING

It has often been found helpful, once the average marks for each session on each scale have been calculated, to rank-order the sessions of a course on each of the scales set out on session assessment forms (Figure 4:2). Thus the sessions can be listed in descending order of their rated enjoyment, information or relevance. This type of layout makes it simple to form a quick overall impression of the results. However, there are dangers in using rank orders as the sole sources of reference about reactions to sessions, for unless the actual scores are also consulted the trainer has no idea of the size of the gap separating particular sessions. When the trainer is appraising the ranked lists he will want to know how wide a margin exists between a session positioned near the bottom of the table and those which come close to the top. For this reason rankings and average scores should be used in combination when reviewing results. Figure 4:2 contained both rank placings and average scores.

In addition the trainer may find there is further information to be obtained if reaction ratings are analysed not only on the basis of treating all trainees as a single group but also after dividing them up in some meaningful way. Thus if members of both line and staff departments are attending the same programme it may be revealing if their reaction ratings are analysed independently, or trainees' reaction material may be divided up in terms of their age.

In some organisations it is customary for speakers to be told the precise ratings given to the sessions that they presented. In situations where a programme is repeated frequently with roughly the same cast on each occasions, this information may motivate speakers to give more attention to the preparation and delivery of their material in an effort to improve on their previous performance.

## A5  KNOWLEDGE QUESTIONNAIRES

So far in this Appendix the construction and use of attitude ratings and session assessment forms have been described. The information they provide is often enough to suggest ways of improving training, but by themselves they may not be sufficient. What may also be required is an indication of how far trainees have learnt what they were intended to learn. Three of the case studies described earlier ( E, F and G) concern the acquisition of knowledge, and in each instance questionnaires were used to assess trainees' improvement. These questionnaires must now be examined to see how they can be developed and used.

Knowledge questionnaires will most often be employed in the form of pre-tests and post-tests - for estimating knowledge before and after training. Clearly knowledge questionnaires must be linked with

G

the original training needs analysis and with the aims of the training programme. The questions asked in a knowledge test should reflect the nature of the information that the trainer wants his students to possess when training is completed; but trainees should not be able to answer most of the questions correctly before training begins. If they cannot answer the questions after training then the course is unsuccessful, but if they can answer them before training it is unnecessary.

KNOWLEDGE GAIN FROM DIFFERENT SPEAKERS
This simple prescription does of course need to be made somewhat more complex. Consider a five-day course with sessions from several different speakers. For the purposes of immediate outcome evaluation an overall estimate is required of knowledge gain (applying to the course as a whole), but for the evaluation information to be usefully fed back for later occasions information is also necessary about the knoweldge gain from different speakers. The course as a whole may have been fairly successful so far as immediate knowledge gain is concerned, but speakers "A" and "F" may have been less than successful in their attempts to get ideas and facts across. Once this is known tactful steps can be taken to improve their sessions.
In other words, questionnaires should be constructed in the light of overall training aims, but the aims of each part of the training must be considered as well. Some criterion questions should, therefore, be included for each segment of training. This brings up the issue of how many questions should be included in a knowledge questionnaire. The answer to this obviously depends on such factors as the type of question, the type of training, the type of trainee, and so on; but as a rough guide it has been found that thirty to forty questions, such as those to be described in the following pages are acceptable to trainers and trainees alike. Time to complete such a number will clearly vary from situation to situation – it should be shorter after training, for example, but a minute for each question is a reasonable average estimate.

CRITERION ITEMS
Summarising these points, the inclusion of criterion items is advised for each session or component part of a training programme. This permits each part to be examined separately, as well as making possible the evaluation of the course as a whole. (The information about knowledge gain in each session could, if the trainer had sufficient time, also be related to information from session assessment forms.) Before turning to more detailed aspects of how to write

questions, there is one further matter to be dealt with: should the same questions serve as a pre-test and as a post-test, or should different items appear in the questionnaire after training?

## RELATION OF PRE-TEST AND POST-TEST QUESTIONS

There is a good argument in favour of making the pre- and post-test items the same. This is recommended for two reasons. The first is practical convenience as it saves the trainer the trouble of drawing up two questionnaires. But the second has a more direct bearing on the training process. If the questions which have been devised are in effect summaries of the core training issues, and obviously this is the idea, the primary goal must be to concentrate upon mastery of these questions. (The nature of the questions will be such that in order to answer them trainees must have learned a good deal; simple rote learning of answers will not suffice.) Some training officers argue that using these items twice makes a training programme look better than it is - since people have seen the "final exam" in advance. But this misses the point, which is that the training does not only look better but that it is better. It is better because using a pre-test is known to increase post-test scores and increased post-test scores are by definition here indicative of better training. Evaluation is primarily to improve training - not simply to measure it afterwards.

But all these arguments hinge upon knowing what the objectives are - that is, upon accurate training-needs assessment - and upon being able to devise items to check whether the aims have been achieved. What sort of items should be used in knowledge questionnaires?

## A6    CONSTRUCTION OF THE QUESTIONNAIRE

Fairly short questions are required, and each should have a generally agreed answer. It is helpful to distinguish between two main types of question - "open-ended" and "restricted choice." Open-ended questions are those which give no clue about the possible answers - the question is left quite "open" - whereas restricted-choice questions present several possible answers, one or more of which is acceptable.

In Figure A3 are four examples of open-ended items drawn from a training questionnaire for junior managers in an airline organisation.

Items of this open-ended type are often appreciated by trainees, but the difficulty for the trainer is sometimes that of making sure that all his questions are objectively scorable.

This difficulty is avoided by restricted-choice questions. Two forms of these may be used. In Figure A4 are two examples of binary-choice questions, and Figure A5 contains four illustrations of multiple-choice questions.

## BINARY- AND MULTIPLE-CHOICE ITEMS

The questions in Figure A4 were used in a study of an industrial relations course for foremen. By "binary-choice" we mean that a trainee has to choose one answer from the two that are provided. An extension of this procedure is to employ multiple-choice items, in which more than two alternative answers are available. It may be that trainees have to indicate which one of the possibilities is correct, or they might have to indicate several correct answers. The first technique (one from many alternatives) is illustrated by items 1 and 2 in Figure A5 (drawn from an engineering foreman's course), and the second approach (several from many alternatives) is shown in items 3 and 4 in that table.

The major advantage of multiple-choice questions is speed of answering as well as of scoring. The major disadvantage is that it is often very difficult to turn course material into a binary- or multiple-choice form. When this can be done only artificially or with difficulty, the open-ended approach is perhaps more acceptable. In general there is no need to strive for all open-ended or all multiple-choice items in a questionnaire – a mixture of types is often easier to construct and more pleasant to answer.

It will be seen from these examples that knowledge questionnaires of the kind advocated here involve short, easily-scored questions. Ease and objectivity of scoring are essential, and it is obviously also vital that the questions should tap the core issues in the training programme.


1       What is the IATP?

2       Name the company's operating divisions

3       What does "latent air potential" mean?

4       What is the difference between CTM and LTM?


FIGURE A3   EXAMPLES OF OPEN-ENDED QUESTIONS

1    Does the company accept the closed-shop principle?

YES
NO

(Tick which is appropriate)

2    Which of the following would you expect the unions to
     negotiate at a national level and which at a local level?

                                        NATIONAL      LOCAL

     Hours of work
     Minimum earnings level
     Rates for particular jobs
     Length of paid holiday
     Maximum hours of overtime working

     (Put ticks in the appropriate column)

FIGURE  A4   EXAMPLES OF BINARY-CHOICE QUESTIONS


ADDITIONAL GUIDELINES FOR CONSTRUCTION OF QUESTIONNAIRE
There are several other guiding points that might assist a reader
who is constructing his own questionnaire. These are most simply
set out as a list:

1    It is helpful if some easy items start the questionnaire. This
     gives trainees some confidence and helps them to get used to
     completing the questionnaire
2    Questions should each carry approximately equal marks. This
     is mainly to ensure that the possible marks obtainable for each
     part of the course are roughly of the same value
3    A question should deal with only one point at a time. It is easy
     to slip into the mistake of asking double questions - for example:
     "What is the latent heat of steam and how is it determined?"
     Two related points may sometimes be presented as two questions,
     but asking only one of these may often be preferable - for
     example: "How is the latent heat of steam determined?"
4    It is essential to avoid ambiguity. This is very easy to say, and
     probably does not appear worth mentioning. But ambiguous
     questions are extremely common in practice. They can be

minimised by trying out a questionnaire before its use – on colleagues or on a sample of people from backgrounds which are similar to those of course members. This preliminary try-out should be standard practice.

5    A related reminder is that in all cases the type of answer required – tick, circle, write a sentence, fill in a blank, and so on – should be clearly indicated on the questionnaire

6    Notice rhat a test with only multiple-choice questions will have a minimum mark obtainable by guessing. This is acceptable, but obtained marks naturally have to be viewed against the "chance" expectation.

## A7 USING AND SCORING A KNOWLEDGE QUESTIONNAIRE

For use as pre-test and post-test the questionnaire clearly has to be administered before and after training. The pre-test administration may take in the first hour of a programme, during which other administrative matters may also be dealt with. It is important to stress to trainees that it is the training which is being tested rather than they. It should also be emphasised that the questionnaire results will not be made available outside the training department as some people are likely to worry that their superior will be informed of their performance. Finally the post-test should be given as soon as possible after the training has been completed and, for the convenience of all concerned. before the trainees disperse.

### THE ALLOCATION OF MARKS

Scoring a knowledge questionnaire is straightforward if the steps described above have been followed. The total marks to be allocated for correct answers might be arranged to total 100, but this is somewhat arbitrary. If a total of 100 is used for about thirty questions, three marks will have to be allocated to most of the questions. This is fairly convenient in that where partly-correct answers are possible these can receive a score of 1 or 2.

When the completed questionnaires have been marked, knowledge gains can be examined in each session as well as over the course as a whole. One possible technique here is to tabulate scores in much the same way as was advocated previously for attitude ratings.

It will be surprising if all sessions are found to be equally successful. Trainers' attention can now be directed to the less-adequate sessions, and attempts can be made to improve these for the next presentation of the course. By these means – as well as by the other evaluation procedures described above – it is possible to develop a self-correcting training system of the kind advocated in the discussion of Case F.

1    The invert level of a drain is:
     (a) The centre line of the drain pipe
     (b) The top outside diameter of the drain pipe
     (c) The top inside diameter of the drain pipe
     (d) The bottom inside diameter of the drain pipe
     (e) The bottom outside diameter of the drain pipe

     (Tick the correct answer)


2    The total area of the holes that should be drilled in a pump
     suction strainer should be equivalent to
     (a) $\frac{1}{2}$ x cross-section area of the pipe
     (b) $1\frac{1}{2}$ x cross-section area of the pipe
     (c) 1 x cross-section area of the pipe

     (Tick the correct answer)


3    In the list below tick those functions which are carried out
     by service departments:
     (a) Supplies
     (b) Maintenance
     (c) Accounting
     (d) Information handling
     (e) Public relations
     (f) Tariffs


4    Tick those of the following jobs which are the responsibility
     of a development engineer
     (a) Designing modifications for aircraft
     (b) Measuring the accuracy of tools and test equipment
     (c) Planning which aircraft are to be overhauled each month
     (d) Forecasting failure rates of components
     (e) Designing tractors
     (f) Agreeing the equipment for new aircraft


FIGURE A5   EXAMPLES OF MULTIPLE-CHOICE QUESTIONS


A8   SHOULD QUESTIONNAIRES BE ANONYMOUS?

When trainees complete questionnaires as part of an evaluation exercise
the problem arises as to whether or not they should be asked to put

their name on the questionnaire form. From the trainer's point of view, being able to identify the sources of completed questionnaires is an advantage as this allows him to make a more thorough analysis of answers than would otherwise be possible. For example, it may enable him to discover which type of trainee benefits most from a particular training programme. However, some evaluators believe that in cases where the trainees' reactions or attitudes are sought, then allowing them to remain anonymous encourages the expression of genuine opinions. And with knowledge questionnaires too, it is conceivable that trainees' co-operation might sometimes be enhanced if anonymity ruled out any possibility of the results of their performance becoming known. There are certainly occasions when such beliefs are justified, and for the trainer to ask for names on questionnaires at such times could adversely affect the quality of the information he collects as well as the relationship between himself and his trainees.

Obviously the trainer must use his own judgement in these situations. One school of thought would advise that, unless the trainer has some purpose in mind which requires his knowing the origin of questionnaires he should not ask for names to be included. And even on occasions when he would like names to be inserted but can see signs that the trainees would prefer not to do this, then the trainer would do best to abide by their wishes. In such circumstances he might ask the trainees instead to add certain relevant information about themselves. This could include, for example, their age – or age range: 21–30, 31–40, and so on – the types of department in which they work or the length of time they have held their present jobs. Such material may be sufficient to permit the trainer to make a more detailed analysis of the material and yet still enable the trainees to remain anonymous.

RELATING PRE- AND POST-TEST PERFORMANCE
When the trainer is carrying out the type of evaluation which requires comparisons of individual pre-test and post-test performance, he will need to be able to identify which two questionnaires were completed by the same trainee. In an investigation of this kind, if trainees want to remain anonymous, the trainer should put a different number on each. of the pre-test forms. Then the questionnaires can be distributed in a random way to the trainees, who are told the purpose of the number and asked to make a note of the one which appears on their form. They can then write this number on their post-test questionnaire when they later complete it. This procedure enables the trainer to sort the collected questionnaires into pre- and post-test pairs answered by the same individual.

# INDEX

# Index